COMMON JOURNEY, DIFFERENT PATHS

COMMON JOURNEY, DIFFERENT PATHS

Spiritual Direction in Cross-Cultural Perspective

*Edited by **Susan Rakoczy, IHM***

ORBIS BOOKS

Maryknoll, New York 10545

The Catholic Foreign Mission Society of America (Maryknoll) recruits and trains people for overseas missionary service. Through Orbis Books, Maryknoll aims to foster the international dialogue that is essential to mission. The books published, however, reflect the opinions of their authors and are not meant to represent the official position of the society.

Copyright © 1992 by Susan Rakoczy
All rights reserved
Published by Orbis Books, Maryknoll, NY 10545
Manufactured in the United States of America

Library of Congress Cataloging-in-Publication Data

Common journey, different paths : spiritual direction in cross-cultural perspective
 / edited by Susan Rakoczy.
     p.   cm.
   Includes bibliographical references.
   ISBN 0-88344-789-4 (pbk.)
   1. Spiritual direction.   2. Intercultural communication.
 I. Rakoczy, Susan.
 BX2350.7.D56 1992
 263.5'3 — dc20
                                        91-40977
                                          CIP

To my parents, Ignatius and Lottie,
with love and gratitude

Contents

Introduction

The world is not as we used to know it, nor is what we know now all that will be in the future. This is certainly true of our contemporary experience, for the advances in communication and transportation have made us a "global village," one whose members encounter the entire gamut of social, political, and economic realities from famine to incredible affluence and prodigal waste of the earth's resources, from oppression to multiparty democracy. Our ecclesial experience during these years of renewal since Vatican II has also given us new and fresh ways to live the Christian life, even while we dream dreams of yet more faithful ways of discipleship.

Renewal has been a time of bringing out from the storeroom things both new and old (Mt. 13:52) as perennial aspects of the Christian experience acquire new depths of meaning as they are practiced in diverse cultures. A very significant stream of renewal these years has been related to prayer, spiritual direction, and retreats, especially the emergence of individually directed retreats. Spiritual direction has, for the most part, lost its previous connotation of one person leading another on the path of discipleship. Instead we now speak of seeking the "direction of the Spirit" together, as one person accompanies another in their faithful response to the Spirit.

Today we are a "world church," one community in Christ on a common journey which yet takes us in distinct and different paths. Spiritual direction has been affected by this experience, since it is no longer unusual for direction to be a conversation of privileged sharing between persons of different cultural backgrounds.

The impetus for this book came first from the five years I spent on the staff of the Centre for Spiritual Renewal in Kumasi, Ghana, giving individually directed and group retreats and accompanying laity, religious, and clergy in spiritual direction. My preparation for and practice of this ministry had been done in the United States, and I found this new setting of working with both Ghanaians and persons from other African countries, Asia, and Europe offering me distinct challenges and wonderful gifts.

During 1988–1989, while on sabbatical at Regis College, Toronto, I focused my research on aspects of faith and culture. As I explored aspects of the cross-cultural experience in prayer and spiritual direction, I found that very little had been published in this area. So the idea for this book took shape, invitations were issued to a wide variety of people around the world to write from their experience (not all of whom, unfortunately, were able to respond), and slowly this volume emerged.

The book is divided into two sections. The first explores the foundations of spiritual direction in cross-cultural perspective and includes essays dealing with intercultural communication, the cognitive dimension of spiritual direction, its external and internal environments, and interpretation of affectivity. The second part speaks of the praxis of direction around the world, with essays from Asia, Latin America, the U.S. Hispanic experience, and Africa. Two concluding articles describe the formation of spiritual directors within an African context and present ways to help directors come to cross-cultural awareness from a Filipino perspective.

My own essay, "Unity, Diversity, and Uniqueness: Foundations of Cross-Cultural Spiritual Direction," explores the meaning of the statement that "Every person is in some respect like all others, like some others, like no other."[1] Lonergan's understanding of the transcultural nature of religious experience undergirds the reflection on the unity of religious experience. Cultural diversity is explored in Western and African cultures with reference to concepts of the self, the world, and God. The uniqueness of each person in the direction dialogue is examined from the perspective of aspects of cross-cultural communication.

Central to spiritual direction is the experience of communication, and this becomes even more significant when two persons attempt to communicate from different backgrounds, worldviews, presuppositions of life, values, and so forth. In her essay, "The Importance of Intercultural Communication Skills," Dr. Marina Herrera discusses some of the crucial dynamics of this process and presents the work of Edward Hall as a significant contribution to this area. She stresses the need to recognize how much communication is nonverbal and therefore the necessity of being able to interpret nonverbal communication in a cross-cultural setting.

The area of faith and freedom in the direction dialogue is explored by Dominic Maruca, SJ, in "Predispositions for Dialogue in Spiritual Direction." He considers the implicit assumptions we may have as we meet with people of different cultures, especially those of cultural and religious superiority. To counteract these, he discusses three principles which can help us "acknowledge [our] latent biases": respecting the uniqueness of each person; cultivating awareness that the cultural and religious gifts each brings are not complete in themselves, thus presenting us with the challenge to learn how to instruct and challenge gently and truthfully; and introducing the truths of life, faith, and prayer according to the needs and growth process of each person.

The article of Anthony J. Gittins, CSSp, "Toward Integral Spirituality: Embodiment, Ecology, and Experience of God," adds the very crucial dimension of relationship to the material world of our bodies, our environment, the physical world. He poses the question of a correlation between types of spiritual experience and the external environment and states, "How variously do different people experience their embodiment? What are the effects of such experience on interpersonal relationships or relations with the wider world? What are some of the different forms of microspirituality and how do they relate to macrospirituality?" A strong microcosm produces a spirituality marked by control, while a weak microcosm leads to a spirituality based on trust, flexibility, vulnerability, and nurturing.

To the presuppositions of cross-cultural spiritual direction already outlined, Gittins reminds us that the person before us brings her or his whole actual world, with all its physical and psychological challenges, to the relationship. To always live near the sea is simply not the same as abiding in the closed environment of a small village near a forest, let alone in an apartment in New York or Tokyo.

Equally absorbing is the world within, that of interiority, which is addressed by Carl F. Starkloff, SJ, in his article "Interiority and the 'Universe of Discourse.'" Using various cultural theorists such as Ruth Benedict, Clifford Geertz, and Robert Lowie, he emphasizes the dimension of symbol as the key to interior experience. Stressing that a knowledge of symbolism in a culture "can deeply affect one's experience in cross-cultural exchange," from his many years of ministry among the native peoples of the United States and Canada, he elaborates this through examples of the use of symbols such as the medicine wheel and sweat lodge. He writes, "Symbols have served to admit us who are otherwise outsiders into the value systems and interior experiences of native people." As we enter with reverence into the symbolic world of sisters and brothers of other cultures, we are more able to listen to the stories of their own journeys in the one Spirit.

One who did this from his monastery and hermitage was Thomas Merton, who only in the last weeks of his life traveled to Asia to experience its spiritual riches. Conrad C. Hoover, CO, develops Merton's approach to spiritual direction in cross-cultural perspective in "Going Deep to the Truth." Important themes from the corpus of Merton's writings, such as searching for the truth, finding our real identity in God, and the unity of humanity's search for God, are highlighted. It is especially the essential unity of the contemplative experience which undergirds the possibility of true cross-cultural encounter in spiritual direction. In this relationship "we can do nothing better than to help others uncover their own identity and destiny as they come to know the Christ who dwells at their center." It is most particularly the experience of "prayerfully and with wonder uncover[ing] Christ in them."

Part two begins with three contributions from Asia. Thomas H. O'Gorman, SJ, focuses on the crucial experience of listening in his piece, "Listening and Spiritual Direction in Asia." He stresses that we must listen to a particular person in a particular context, the ways the depth and diversity of Asian experience are able to affect the listening process, and possible patterns of response in listening. Included is discussion of the crucial need for awareness of the social aspects of our faith as they emerge in the direction dialogue.

Lily Quintos, rc, describes how the worldviews of the Asian religions of Buddhism, Confucianism, and Taoism appear in the religious experience of Asian persons in the First Week of the Spiritual Exercises in her essay "Experiences of the Heart: The Spiritual Exercises across Cultures." She presents the Buddhist concept of "indifference," the Confucian understanding of human nature, and the Taoist views of sin and harmony as emerging in the prayer experiences of Asian exercitants.

Joan Conrad, SSND, brings twenty-eight years of experience in Japan to her article, "Spiritual Direction in Japan." Describing her experiences of retreats and spiritual direction, including longer formation experiences, she writes, "we have discovered that when a person prays contemplatively, this person begins to meet within himself or herself responses that are both individual and may also be universal."

Latin America is represented by articles from Brazil and Chile. Padraic Leonard, CSSp, writes in "Spiritual Direction and Religious Experience in the Cultural Environment of Brazil" of the richness of the diversity of Brazilian cultural experience. Examples drawn from spiritual direction and retreats highlight the depth of the religious spirit of the many groups which form the Brazilian people. Especially significant is his description of the emerging spirituality of the Brazilian poor and how it affects spiritual direction, especially in a group setting.

Ann Belliveau, SSA, who has ministered in Chile for over ten years, describes some of the challenges faced by a spiritual director in a country emerging from years of political oppression in "Spiritual Direction in Chile: Confronting the Experience of Oppression." She stresses the need to help Chileans learn how to bring their religious experience to reflective awareness, describing discernment of the experience of inner freedom of the person as especially significant. Two aspects of Latin American culture, male machismo and women's poor self-image, are presented as especially important cultural facts in the spiritual direction process.

Spiritual direction within the U.S. Hispanic experience is discussed by Adele J. Gonzalez in "Companion on Pilgrimage: The Hispanic Experience." The richness of Hispanic values such as respect for the person, love of family, intense sense of community, an appreciation of the present moment, and the celebration of life are described in relation to the religious experience of the Hispanic people she has directed. Ms. Gonzalez, herself Hispanic, has also discovered how crucial are group and informal experiences of spiritual direction among these members of the Christian community.

Two contributions from Africa explore the use of dreams and imagination in prayer and spiritual direction. Bernard Ward, MCCJ, who has had extensive pastoral experience in Malawi and now in South Africa, discusses "Using Dreams and Imagination" and describes situations from directed retreats in which the use of "dreams and images can be a way of bridging the cultural gap. The image speaks where language fails." The examples given from directed retreat situations and spiritual direction sessions depict how persons can be aided in using images and their dreams as ways of deeper encounter with God. Such use is also therapeutic in the broadest view as persons begin to face some of their conflicts in a context which is both nonthreatening and life enhancing. In the end, what is most important is that "they meet Christ as one like themselves rather than as a foreigner."

Gregory Lourens of Cape Town, South Africa, explores the topic of "Finding Identity in South Africa's Apartheid Society" through the exposition and analysis of a long-term direction relationship with a "so-called coloured" woman who, through prayer and dream analysis, makes a painful and life-giving journey to self-acceptance and self-affirmation.

Two concluding articles from African and Asian contexts provide us with directions and suggestions in helping spiritual direction to become truly cross-cultural. Terrence P. Charlton, SJ, contributes "Forming Spiritual Directors in Ghana," which describes a four-phase experience for the formation of directors, using limited personnel and material resources, developed by the staff of the Centre for Spiritual Renewal in Kumasi, Ghana. The four workshops of varying lengths integrate prayer, life journey, discernment and decision making, counseling skills and spiritual direction formation within a context based on the Spiritual Exercises of St. Ignatius and the gifts of African culture.

In "Toward a Multicultural Approach to Spiritual Direction," Judette Gallares, rc, of the Philippines offers three areas for consideration to develop educational and formation programs for spiritual directors working in multicultural settings. She focuses on inculturation, which includes experiencing the popular religion of the people to enter more fully into their cultural milieu and on multicultural psycho-spiritual processes, which embrace a discussion of "transference" and "countertransference" in cross-cultural understanding; she also offers suggestions for multicultural communication exercises for both directors and directees and/or retreatants.

I would like to thank all those who encouraged me to begin and continue the work of bringing this book to life: my colleagues at Regis during the year I spent with them, especially Margaret Brennan, IHM, and Carl Starkloff, SJ; my editor at Orbis, Bill Burrows, who was so easily persuaded of the need for a book of this kind and who has patiently accompanied me as we worked together, half a world apart; to all the contributors for their creativity and cooperation; to the IHM Community in South Africa, whose support has been so important and life-giving; and to my friends and colleagues at St. Joseph's Theological Institute, whose curious interest in this project helped keep me going.

May 31, 1991
Feast of the Visitation

NOTES

1. Clyde Kluckhohn and Henry A. Murray, *Personality in Nature, Society and Culture* (New York: Alfred A. Knopf, 1948), p. 53.

Part I

Foundational Issues

1

Unity, Diversity, and Uniqueness: Foundations of Cross-Cultural Spiritual Direction

SUSAN RAKOCZY, IHM

Spiritual direction is a privileged meeting of hearts. Built on trust in the bond of the Spirit of God, two persons come together in faith to hear the story of the workings of the Spirit in the life of one of them. For the person who shares her or his experience of God, there is always the moment of "stepping out on the water" as one begins to speak of what is most sacred in life. The listener, who is companion on the journey, is called to receive that sharing in trust and love, with encouragement and support, and, at times, with the invitation of challenge to further growth, even at the cost of pain and suffering.

Such sharing and listening demand much from both persons in the direction dialogue. Trust, openness, confidence, awareness, and sensitivity to the ways of the Spirit in one's heart allow the person to reveal the depths of the mystery of God in his or her life. The director or companion waits in readiness to receive this intimate revelation, to respond with wisdom, discernment, and love to what has been shared in order that both may see more clearly the direction[1] in which the Spirit is leading.

This is a very demanding experience for both persons, even when they are of the same culture and religious background. It is no easy experience to begin a new direction relationship, to share something of one's graced history, to learn to trust a new companion in the Spirit. And for the director, each person who comes to share a journey is a unique gift of God whose sharing provides a new opportunity in which to learn more profoundly how to listen and respond in the Spirit.

But in our world church today, the direction experience often takes place between persons of different cultures and backgrounds. Even when they share the same culture, they may be of different economic and social back-grounds. The same challenges apply when a woman and a man come together in the direction experience. On what common bases can such intimate sharing be fruitful if life experiences, language and culture, values and thought patterns are different?

It has been said that "Every person is in some respect like all others, like some others, like no other" (Kluckhohn and Murray 1948:53). This triad of commonality, group identity, and uniqueness provides us with a structure in which to explore some of the theological, cultural, and psychological foundations for spiritual direction in cross-cultural perspective.

"LIKE ALL OTHERS"

The contribution of Bernard Lonergan to foundational issues of theology and theological method is well known and has helped to undergird the contemporary emphasis in spirituality on explorations of interiority and religious experience.[2]

Lonergan's analysis has exposed the framework of a transcendental method in which the human activities of attention to experience, under-standing what has been experienced, judging in the light of understanding, and deciding in terms of what has been understood form the structure of human consciousness (1972:6–20). These four moments of intentionality describe a conscious movement in which, as we move from level to level, the self becomes ever more aware of itself in distinctly different ways.

The empirical level of consciousness in which "something" is sensed, perceived, imagined, felt, or heard is that of experience. Intellectually we attempt to understand and gain insight into what has been experienced. We then search for the truth of what we understand and finally move to action as we responsibly deliberate on what to do. These operations are conscious, dynamic, unified, and invariant. As a method they move us along the path of desire from what is unknown to the known.

Vernon Gregson has observed that "Desire, its struggle and its triumphs, is the clue to Lonergan, and not any desire, but your own desire, and my own, and his" (Gregson 1988:17). It is the force of what we truly want that shapes our lives. Certainly a core dimension of spiritual direction is the exploration of one's deepest desires in God.

Lonergan was a North American, trained in Western philosophical and theological traditions, who worked within that perspective. However, he asserts that the transcendental method is transcultural and thus describes the basic human operations of intentionality of all persons. He states:

> Clearly it [transcendental method] is not transcultural inasmuch as it is explic-itly formulated. But it is transcultural in the realities to which the formulation refers, for these realities are not the product of any culture, but, on the contrary, the principles that produce cultures, preserve them, develop them (1972:282).

In other words, the description of this method stems from Lonergan's own Western tradition and so its form is not transcultural. For example, to ask "How do I know what I know and how do I know that?" flows from Western philosophical concerns. But Lonergan maintains that all people of all cultures move from desire to knowledge to action along the same pathways, even when they speak of how they do this in distinct and different ways.

This very brief exposition of transcendental method as transcultural helps us to explore the common aspects of religious experience. If each of us is in some respects "like all others," how can we describe that in religious language? Again Lonergan's reflections are of great help in understanding this dimension of experience.

Lonergan places religion within the fourth level of human awareness, that of decision making and of love (1972:104–5). Experience relates to the first level of consciousness, of the awareness of what is happening to us, around us, within us. Linking these two dimensions provides us with an understanding of religious experience which "means personal consciousness of being drawn toward the ultimate" (Gregson 1985:60).

The ultimate is expressed in theistic language, and Lonergan states that "being in love with God is the basic fulfillment of our conscious intentionality" (1972:105). In beautiful and emotionally charged language, he speaks of this experience in the words of self-surrender, of love without limits that transforms the person. Echoing the language of Scripture, he speaks of radical peace, the gift of love given in the Spirit, of a love of neighbor that radically reorientates the person from selfishness to self-giving.

Because Lonergan was a Catholic theologian, the question now must be asked if his analysis bears any relationship to the experience of other religions or whether it is exclusively Christian. He asserted its universal nature, using the work of the historian of religions Friedrich Heiler, who described seven common areas of religious experience: the existence of transcendent reality and its immanence in human hearts; this reality as supreme beauty, truth, righteousness, and goodness and also love, mercy, and compassion; that persons find the way to this reality through repentance and prayer and also through love of neighbor, including enemies; and that the goal of the way is knowledge, union, or dissolution in this reality (1972:109).

The gift of God's love is transcultural in itself, though its manifestations are diverse. It is "not restricted to any stage or section of human culture but rather is the principle that introduces a dimension of other-worldliness into any culture" (1972:283). The experience of God's love is then the inner core of all religious experience. It is the common language that we speak to one another when we speak of the experience of God as Holy Mystery, though our languages and thought patterns may differ.

Lonergan further distinguishes between the inner and outer determinants of this experience. The inner determinants are the gift of God's transforming love and human response and consent to it. The outer determinants are the expressions of this experience through the accumulated wisdom and experience of a religious tradition (1972:289).

Another way to speak of this relationship is in terms of "infrastructure" and "suprastructure" (Lonergan 1985:70–71). The core experience that is the infrastructure of all religious experience is being in love in an unrestricted fashion. But such experience, while conscious and transformative of the depths of the human heart, must be thematized and expressed.

Here we see emerging the distinctiveness in the world religions of the interpretation of this core experience. Religious language, employed in a variety of ways such as prayer, sacred writings, belief statements, and so forth, provides ways to symbolize the suprastructure of the inner, transcultural dimension.

In Christian language, we can use Paul's description of God's love flooding our heart through the Holy Spirit who has been given to us (Rom. 5:5) to express the infrastructure. Other religions would use other formulations. Christian suprastructure speaks of this Spirit as that of Jesus, who was sent by the Creator for the sake of the salvation of the world (Jn. 3:16) and who through his death and resurrection has given humanity new life in the Spirit, forming women and men in community in that Spirit and empowering them for mission and ministry in the steps of Jesus.

This description and analysis of Lonergan's transcendental method as the invariant structure of human consciousness, understanding, judgment, and decision making, coupled with his assertion that the experience of unrestricted love is the fulfillment of our deepest longings, provide us with ways to affirm that as human beings we are indeed "like all others." In the experience of cross-cultural spiritual direction, whether between persons of distinct religious traditions (Buddhist-Christian), different emphases within the same tradition (Catholic-Methodist), other cultures (European-Asian), or a woman-man relationship, we can begin confident of this common basis in our humanity: We are all searching for something beyond ourselves and that "something" is the experience of unrestricted and unbounded love.

"LIKE SOME OTHERS"

As human beings we are distinctively "like some others" because we are shaped and formed from our earliest moments by our cultural experience. Myriad definitions and descriptions of culture abound,[3] but for our purposes we can work within the parameters of an understanding in which culture means the ways a group of people has organized all aspects of its life (physical, psychological, social, religious, economic, and so forth) in order to meet its needs and allow it to confront successfully the challenges presented to it by life.

Through the process of "enculturation" (sometimes termed "socialization"), persons from their earliest years learn the way of life which is the pattern of their culture. Much of what is learned is absorbed informally and in a sense unconsciously, so that the ways "we" do things become second nature and common sense to the person.[4] Physical habits, ways of social organization (family, clan, tribe), roles of women and men, economic and political relationships, and approaches to the transcendent all reflect the distinct worldview of that culture. Luzbetak states: "A world view represents the deepest questions one might ask about the world and life, and about the corresponding orientation that one should take toward them" (1988:252).

These questions focus on the nature of the world, the person, the meaning of life, the relationship of the person to the world and to other persons, the basic values of life, how to live successfully and what makes a person happy or satisfied, the possibility of life after death. These are obviously the basic philosophical questions which human beings have wrestled with since the beginning of time. Cultures answer them in distinct and different ways, and here lies the basis of the assertion that all of us are "like some others," since we think and act from our own set of cultural assumptions, norms, and values constantly and consistently.

It is only when we have an experience of cross-cultural encounter that jars our cultural sensibilities somewhat that we say, "How strange these people are; why don't they do things the way we do?" The severe form of this experience is known as "culture shock," in which entry into a new culture is disorienting in a considerable measure and the person feels as if the solid ground underfoot is no longer there, since many or all of their cultural assumptions and values are now being daily challenged by entirely new patterns of life and thought.

My own cross-cultural experience is in Africa; I spent nearly six years in the West African country of Ghana and now am ministering in South Africa. Reflection on the distinctively different African views of the self, the world, and religion in contrast to the Western worldview can provide a good illustration of the challenges presented in the spiritual direction experience when persons of different cultural experiences meet to share the deepest movements of the human spirit in God.

In the West, especially from the time of the Enlightenment, the self has been understood as a distinct individual, with unique value and distinct rights. Persons have the right to make something of their lives, to take responsibility for their life direction, to use their talents and gifts to the full. Such emphasis puts supreme value on the right of self-determination, self-achievement, self-satisfaction.

Such personal responsibility for the shaping of one's life is a good and flows from the Judeo-Christian understanding of the dignity and worth of each human being. What is weak in this dimension of worldview is the bonding of the person with the community. Especially in this century and particularly in American culture, individual self-determination has been exalted over the needs of the community, giving rise to an "individualism" which found its most skewed expression in the "Me Generation"—my needs above all else. This cultural value has profoundly influenced all facets of life, including politics, economics, and religion.[5]

When a Western person, formed in this worldview of the importance of the person and his or her rights and responsibilities, meets an African in the direction relationship, they meet someone whose experience of the self is distinctly different. In contrast to the West, the African individual does not exist apart from the community. The classic phrasing of this intrinsic relationship comes from John Mbiti: "I am, because we are; and since we are, therefore I am" (Mbiti 1969:108–9).

The person is part of the whole, and one's identity flows from the corporate experience and never in isolation from it, since "it is the community which defines who he/she is and who he/she can become" (Ray 1976:132). The uniqueness of each person is affirmed and acknowledged, but one's own individuality and freedom "are always balanced by destiny and community" (ibid.).

The various initiation rites that have been and, to a certain extent, still remain so important in various African cultures, integrate the person into the society so that she or he finds their identity within it. This continues beyond death, since ancestors are regarded as intrinsically part of the community, able to influence events and guide the community. Life is one continuous movement of social experience from birth to death.

The emphasis in moral behavior flows from the community to the person; the individual becomes conscious, through social interaction, of what is expected in terms of right and wrong, cultural norms and responsibilities, rights and privileges. One acts therefore in concert with the group and not apart from it. When good is done, it is good for the group, and when evil is committed, the shame affects the whole community.

Although Western influences of various kinds are profoundly affecting African society, this experience of the self in community remains the foundation of African self-understanding. It is clear, then, what misunderstandings can easily occur in spiritual direction and other helping relationships when a Western director urges Africans to assume a degree of self-consciousness and self-assertion for which their cultural experience has not prepared them. At the same time, the distinct values of both worldviews can enrich each other, the Western person learning the value of community experience as formative of the person, and the African coming to a deeper awareness of her or his unique personal goodness and worth.

Understanding the world is also distinctly different in Western and African worldviews. Much has been written recently about Western abuse of the environment as stemming from a perversion of the biblical mandate to "fill the earth and subdue it" (Gen. 1:28) and the need for a spirituality that will form persons and communities in care and concern for our earth.[6] The person stands over and against creation in all its dimensions, using and abusing it for one's own ends.

Key to this Western worldview is the separation of the person and the community from the world of nature. Domination best describes this stance in which nature is made the servant of human needs, wants, and desires. The exaltation of the uniqueness and goodness of humanity is seen in discontinuity with the goodness and value of all the other facets of creation. Humanity and the rest of creation are in a relationship of ruler to servant, rather than of interdependence which acknowledges the truth that the earth provides humanity with its basic sustenance — air, water, food, and so forth — and thus the human community is called to steward it faithfully and carefully.

The African experience is again decidedly and strikingly different. In the same way as we have seen that the person is vitally and organically bonded in community with others, so also is this union extended to all of creation. The African worldview shares with the Judeo-Christian tradition the understanding of God as Creator of the material universe (Mbiti 1969:39–41). Nature in all its dimensions is alive with the presence of God, and communities and their members experience God in and through creation.

In contrast to the Western mode of domination, the African strives to live in harmony with nature. The various facets of creation — the sky, the sun and moon, mountains, forests and trees, rivers and water, plants and animals — all have at least implicit religious meaning and often explicit significance.

Throughout Africa the transcendence of God is strongly stressed, and God's immanence is understood to be experienced through creation. Different groups, such as the Ashanti of Ghana, speak of various "small gods" (*abosom*) or minor divinities that are associated with natural phenomena such as lakes, rivers, trees, and so on. John Pobee points out that "the gods are not the stone or tree or river itself, but that they may from time to time be contacted at a concrete habitation, though they are not confined therein" (Pobee 1979:47).

All of creation is charged with the presence of the invisible: God and the spirit world, both good and evil, and so it is said that "African peoples 'see' that invisible universe when they look at, hear or feel the visible and tangible world" (Mbiti 1969:57). A universe alive with power generates both fear and awe, and therefore also characteristic of the African approach to the world is the desire to live in harmony with it, not apart from it, together with fear of the spirits that dwell in the forest, bush, and rivers. Mbiti states that "People report that they see the spirits in ponds, caves, groves, mountains or outside their villages, dancing, singing, herding cattle, working in their fields or nursing their children" (1969:81).

The spirits can communicate with persons through dreams, visions, and mediums. The relationships vary with each African society, but the sense of the presence of the spirits is pervasive for both Christians and traditional believers. The spirits are linked with the ancestors, and "bad spirits" are often understood to be those who have not been accepted into the "community of ancestors" because of the way they lived on earth. Now they cause problems for their families here. A Ghanaian priest I knew once prayed in the liturgy in thanksgiving "for delivering [him] from the fear of evil spirits." He was not denying the existence and activity of such spirits but rather their power over him.

All of these elements of the African view of the world and creation thus are distinctly different in many ways from the Western perspective. The African person in the situation of spiritual direction, whether as director or directee, brings to this sacred relationship the experience of harmony with nature, a lack of domineering attitude toward it, a sense of the invisible world alive in the visible, and a strong conviction that various spirits can communicate with the person and the community. These challenge Western perceptions of the secularity of the universe, a sense of control over it, and at least a great skepticism about the existence of any kinds of spirits or similar beings with power to influence human behavior (notwithstanding the contributions of modern psychology, which has shown us that we are far more complex than we had dreamed).

Different also are Western and African understandings of religion and its relation to life. During the past several hundred years religious belief, practice, and experience have become an option for Western persons and not a core way to organize life experience. For those who remain believers, too often religion is a separate compartment of life, with various religious duties to be "done" but with little influence on ordinary life other than the vague desire to do good and respect the rights of others. One attends church on Sunday and then gives little thought to religious commitment the rest of the week.

Organized religion in the West has seen its influence decline in many ways as this dichotomy between the religious and the secular has become more pronounced. Even the rise of various fundamentalist groups has not challenged this approach, since personal faith is seen as operative in a fairly narrow, restricted sphere with little social or political implication for the wider society.

The Western person brings much of this perspective to spiritual direction when the matter to be discussed is only that which is "religious." Prayer experience is important, but one's involvement with a local political party is not. Any approach or suggestion that reinforces this dichotomy in Western experience between "religion" and "life" widens the gap.

African experience is radically different, for "religion is seen as inseparable from African culture" (Twesigye 1987:84). In African traditional religions, formal distinctions between the sacred and the secular, the spiritual and the material dimensions of life, do not exist. Life and religious expression are one, since the invisible world of the sacred is so intimately linked with ordinary life. The universe is basically a religious universe.

Traditional African religious experience is thus a daily affair, permeating every aspect of life: rising; getting water; cooking food; going to the farm, office, or school; attending a funeral or wedding; drinking beer with friends. Certain religious rituals surround specific life events such as birth and death, but the African religious worldview is broader, since it encompasses all that is human and part of life.

The African who becomes a Christian or Moslem or follower of any other world religion looks for an experience of religion that also encompasses their whole life: language, thought patterns, social relationships, attitudes, values, desires, fears. It is not enough to "do religious things" regularly, since their desire is for a religious worldview that will fill the world with meaning and be especially sustaining in times of fear and crisis.

In the situation of spiritual direction, the African person brings her or his desire that experience of God be found in every facet of life without exception. Western directors or directees, formed in the pattern of religion as one part of life, can be disconcerted by the wholistic view presented by their African brothers or sisters, but they have much to gain from it.

We have seen through comparison of the Western and African views of self, the world, and religion, that all persons are "like some others" since they are formed in the worldview of their culture. This worldview is as pervasive as the air one breathes, and it is often only through either direct cross-cultural experience or vicariously through study of other cultures that one begins to realize that the "oxygen content" of one's particular kind of cultural air is a bit different from that of the sister or brother of another culture. Sensitivity to the differences of worldviews one meets in the spiritual direction relationship is thus a prerequisite for fruitful, grace-filled sharing and discernment in the one Spirit of God.

"LIKE NO OTHER"

The person who comes seeking support, affirmation, encouragement, and challenge in the journey of faith is unique in all of creation. The search for Holy Mystery that joins them with all other people and the common cultural experience that bonds them with a particular group provide them with fundamental grounding points in life experience. Yet the call of God to each heart is distinct and never to be repeated. No matter how often an experienced director begins with a new person, nothing can be assumed or taken for granted, because the pathways of grace are always the person's alone. We are on "holy ground," indeed, as we hear the story of grace told in new forms and new themes.

How can the director, conscious of the common bases of religious experience and the distinctiveness of particular cultural worldviews, meet people in their uniqueness and be present to them with all the grace and attentiveness that we see Jesus meeting people in the Gospels? David Augsburger has described a triad of responses that allow one person to enter the "world" of another (Augsburger 1986:27–37). Each of them—sympathy, empathy, and "interpathy" — is a progressively deeper experience of presence and psychological-spiritual bonding with people who come in all their uniqueness. The first two are well-known categories. It is his description of "interpathy" that provides a new and very helpful type of response.

Augsburger uses the image of frame and picture to describe the relationship of persons in each type of response (1986:31). Sympathy "is the spontaneous response to another's emotional experience" (1986:27) in which one projects one's feelings upon another. For example, one says to a friend whose father has died, "I know just how you feel." Of course she doesn't, but words of sympathy do help a bit to alleviate the pain. In the sympathetic response, the counselor or director is both frame and picture, for she or he judges the other in terms of their own feelings, not the feelings of the one in pain and distress.

The empathetic response is deeper, for one shares another's feelings through compassionate active imagination. I choose to enter into the experience of another in order to share the pain or the joy, the anxiety or the peace, but "I do not own it; I share it. My experience is the frame, your pain the picture" (1986:31).

"Interpathy" allows the director or counselor to enter the world of others in their uniqueness. Augsburger describes the experience as both cognitive and affective:

> Interpathy is an intentional cognitive envisioning and affective experiencing of another's thoughts and feelings, even though the thoughts rise from another process of knowing, the values grow from another frame of moral reasoning, and the feelings spring from another basis of assumptions (1986:29).

It is an experience of "feeling with" and "thinking with" the other. I try to believe, feel, and think as this person does. Her or his experience becomes both frame and picture for me. If I am an Irish male Roman Catholic priest directing a Kenyan married woman who is very active in her parish, I am challenged to think and feel "African, female, lay, and married" in order to hear and respond to the ways she is experiencing and responding to the Spirit of God.

My own experience is set aside as I try to enter into the worldview and consciousness of the other. I welcome the other's values and ways of knowing and deciding and listen to her experience within that frame and picture which is hers. Of course, I do not become her or definitively assume her values and worldview as my own, but her experience becomes the center of the direction or counseling encounter. However, the director needs to maintain a certain critical consciousness of the new worldview in the interpathic experience, since "Every culture has aspects of it that need redemption. Oftentimes an 'outsider' can see better than the 'insider' the culture's blind spots and potentials" (Gallares 1990:76).

Interpathy requires both courage and attentive presence on the part of the director. To leave behind, however briefly, one's own cultural supports and enter the world of the other is a daunting prospect. It is an entry into the unknown which both invites and frightens. John Dunne describes this experience as "passing over and coming back":

> Passing over is a shifting of standpoint, a going over to the standpoint of another culture, another way of life, another religion. It is followed by an equal and opposite process we might call "coming back," coming back with new insight to one's own culture, one's own way of life, one's own religion (1972:ix).

One returns changed by the experience of entering into new thought and feeling patterns that challenge the way one has always thought and felt. This process of dying to oneself, however briefly, in the interpathic encounter hopefully leads to the new life of new understanding, vision, and bonding with the sister or brother of another cultural experience.

Interpathy is grounded in personal presence to the other before me. Augsburger stresses that "In cross-cultural pastoral counseling, the greatest gift the counselor may have to offer is the opening of the self to receive another in authentic presence" (1986:37). To be fully present to another means first to be fully present to myself, to be aware of the twists and turns of my own spiritual journey, my patterns of strength and weakness, my hopes and concerns. It requires the courage to enter fully the experience of conversion which is the Gospel call to radical transformation and healing of the self in God.

To listen to another with authentic presence demands an openness from the very center of one's being, which is in God. Their own journey and experience becomes the center of my world now; indeed, becomes my world, however briefly. As I listen to the unique and wonderful and painful stories of others who are also searching for wholeness and transformation and grace, each in their own way, all that I have experienced in my own journey becomes available to them, insofar as I am truly present to them.

This happens not so much through sharing my own experience (though that has its place at times) but in the meeting of one person with another in the bonding grace that is the one Spirit of God alive in each heart, in each culture, in all humanity. I am there for and with the other with my whole being, and nothing is more important at this moment than my complete presence to her or him.

This is a very difficult and challenging experience and is impeded by the reality of sin, weakness, and bias in the director's heart. Bias is both an intellectual and affective distortion of the mind and heart which blocks cognitive, moral, and affective conversion.[7] Bias generates obscurity, bewilderment, doubt, insecurity, and disquiet as one meets the other.

The director's own self-awareness is continuously challenged in the cross-cultural experience. She or he must ask questions such as: To what in the other's worldview, image of God, self, and community, am I not open? When they speak of aspects of their cultural experience, why do I experience disquiet? Is it because it is simply "different," or is it because of a lack of openness on my part? How free am I to listen with all my heart to their experience? How does my own cultural experience impede my listening, i.e., a Western woman listening to an African priest justify the sexism of his culture? Why do I fear the challenge of "interpathy" and the "crossing over" this demands? What in me needs to die so that new life can come forth in the direction relationship?

Bias and its opposite — freedom — need to be consciously addressed by both persons in the direction relationship. The directee may not feel comfortable with a person of another culture whose manner of eye contact, address, and dialogue are very much shaped by the other's cultural experience. For example, in my experience of direction in Africa, I have learned that many Africans will not look one straight in the eyes; this is not lack of courtesy but the polite form of presence for them. Americans, however, expect people to look directly at them.

Insofar as the director is aware of the dimensions of bias in her or his own heart, such as racism and racist attitudes, they are more able to be fully present to the directee, and their responses, both cognitive and affective, will be freer and less limited by bias.

Another area that is important to consider is the expectations of the directee. What do I expect to hear, and what do I do when I hear something else? When I ministered in Ghana at a retreat center, I usually asked people at the beginning of their retreat what they wanted from the days of prayer. Often I would be told, "I want God to solve all my problems." This was at first disconcerting to me, since I had expected some comment such as "I want to grow in prayer" or "I want to come closer to God." But I learned that for the Ghanaian, God was seen as the "problem solver" who would lessen suffering and make life easier. As a director I needed to honor this initial desire even as I tried to help people widen their image of God and expectation of God's action in their lives so they could deepen their relationship with God even when "all their problems were not solved" in a few days of retreat.

Another area of interpathy and freedom is in listening to dreams and experiences of ghosts, spirits, and witches. The Western director is probably open to some areas of dream interpretation from the study of Jung and others. But the "spirit" world is a new experience. Interpathy requires that I "see and hear the ghost or spirit" with the person, listening at many different levels in order to help them interpret their experience and relate it to the action of God in their lives. Fear is often the dominant feeling in such sharing, and it is crucial that the director not soothe the fear too quickly out of her or his own needs but help people to discover the God who loves them in the midst of that fear.

The director's task is also to aid the person in understanding that this "spirit," as an experience of fear and dread, is a symbolic way of dealing with internal tensions, conflicts, struggles, and incompatibilities.[8] The symbols that are important to the person, such as those for God, evil, sin, fear, hope, love, and so on, "have to be transformed before they then can be reliable guides" (Kiely 1982:134). Symbols arise out of images and feelings, and this transformation process, which always respects the integrity of the person's experience, strives to help the person discover the meaning in the symbol so that he or she can more consciously respond to God present in that experience.

Both director and directee are thus "like no other" as they walk the journey of faith together. Sharing the universal experience of human nature and gifted with distinct cultural worldviews, they strive to hear and listen to one another as the persons they are, with all their gifts and strengths, limits and weaknesses. The approach of interpathy challenges the director to cross the barrier of difference and assume new ways of thinking and feeling, however briefly and incompletely, in order to be with the person in compassionate presence, which leads to greater life and greater growth in the Spirit of God.

CONCLUSION

This essay has been an exploration of the meaning of the reality that all human persons are like all others, like some others, and yet each is truly unique. Using Bernard Lonergan's analysis of the structure of human consciousness and his assertion that the search for the ultimate, known and experienced as God in religious language, is common to all, we established the grounding point of an understanding of the transcultural nature of religious experience.

Each woman and man is "like some others" because of her or his distinct cultural experience. A brief exposition of the contrasts between Western and African views of the self, the world, and religion provided one way to describe the richness of the human experience as it reflects on basic realities.

To meet and be present to the uniqueness of each person in the spiritual direction relationship is an immense challenge, especially as one begins to understand how culture shapes each of us. David Augsburger's concept of interpathy furnished a very workable category in which to describe the quality of presence that is so vital in the direction relationship. More than meeting people as they are in their uniqueness, the director is challenged to be "as they are," for example, black, poor, female, Asian in thought and feeling, as she or he listens to the ways of God in the other's heart.

These theological, cultural, and psychological concepts provide a solid foundation for analysis of the spiritual direction relationship as it is experienced in cross-cultural perspective. They give both director and directee a prism that refracts the cross-cultural relationship into its elemental parts without destroying its unity. That unity is the one Spirit of God, experienced in wonderful diversity in human hearts in all the countries and cultures of our earth as persons seek persistently for the ways of God and the presence of God in their lives.

NOTES

1. In the contemporary literature of spiritual direction, the meaning of "direction" has shifted from the traditional perspective of one person showing another the path of God's ways to both seeking the forward direction of the Spirit together. The "director" is seen as empathetic companion on the journey. Cf. William Barry and William Connolly, *The Practice of Spiritual Direction* (New York: Seabury Press, 1982), which describes spiritual direction as the "help given by one Christian to another that enables that person to pay attention to God's personal communication to him or her, to respond to this personally communicating God, to grow in intimacy with this God, and to live out the consequences of the relationship" (p. 8). Kathleen Fischer, in *Women at the Well: Feminist Perspectives in Spiritual Direction* (New York: Paulist Press, 1988), stresses that the direction relationship focuses on "awareness of and response to God in one's life" (p. 3).

2. Louis Dupre's study of religious experience, *The Other Dimension* (Garden City, N.Y.: Doubleday and Co., Inc., 1972) explores the meaning of religious faith and human experience. The works of Sebastian Moore are also a significant contribution to this area: *The Crucified Jesus Is No Stranger* (New York: Seabury, 1977); *The Fire and the Rose Are One* (New York: Seabury, 1980); *The Inner Loneliness* (New York: Crossroad, 1982); and *Let This Mind Be in You* (New York: Harper & Row, 1985).

3. Louis J. Luzbetak provides a comprehensive overview of diverse understandings of culture in his chapter on "The Nature of Culture" in *The Church and Cultures* (Maryknoll, N.Y.: Orbis Books, 1988), pp. 133–222. He describes culture as "society's design for living" and includes these elements as central to this design: "(1) a *plan* (2) consisting of a set of *norms, standards* and associated *notions* and *beliefs* (3) for *coping* with the various demands of life, (4) shared by a *social group,* (5) *learned* by the individual from the society, and (6) organized into a *dynamic* (7) *system* of control" (p. 157).

4. Luzbetak gives many fascinating examples of the ways we take things for granted in our cultures in terms of food, personal habits, thought patterns, etc., in his work. *See* pp. 182–222.

5. Robert Bellah's *Habits of the Heart* (University of California Press, 1988) provides a comprehensive analysis of individualism in American culture and its implications for community and commitment.

6. During this time of ecological crisis, there is a retrieval of the Christian tradition of reverence for creation and a reinterpretation of it. The works of Thomas Berry and Matthew Fox are important sources. *See especially* Anne Lonergan and Caroline Richards, *Thomas Berry and the New Cosmology* (Mystic, Conn.: Twenty-Third Publications, 1987) and Fox's *Original Blessing* (Sante Fe, N. M.: Bear & Co., 1983). Also important is Sean McDonagh's *To Care for the Earth: A Call to a New Theology* (Santa Fe, N. M.: Bear & Co., 1987). An overview of "Creational Spiri-

tuality" was done by Thomas E. Clarke in *The Way* 29 (January 1989): 68–80.

7. Lonergan treats bias fully and extensively. *See Insight: A Study in Human Understanding* (London: Darton, Longman & Todd, 1957), pp. 191–206, 218–42, and *Method*, pp. 53, 217, 230–31, 240, 270, 284.

8. Lonergan describes a symbol as "an image of a real or imaginary object that evokes a feeling (*Method*, p. 66.) At issue here is not the reality of the ghost or spirit but the response to it, since the fear and dread are real.

REFERENCES

Augsburger, David W. (1986). *Pastoral Counseling Across Cultures.* Philadelphia: The Westminster Press.

Dunne, John S. (1972). *The Way of All the Earth: Experiments in Truth and Religion.* New York: MacMillan Publishing Co.

Gallares, Josephine B. (1990). "A Multicultural Approach to the Ministry of Retreats and Spiritual Direction." M.A. thesis, Fordham University.

Gregson, Vernon. (1985). *Lonergan, Spirituality and the Meeting of Religions.* New York: University Press of America.

———. (1988). "The Desire to Know: Intellectual Conversion." In Vernon Gregson, ed. *The Desires of the Human Heart.* New York: Paulist Press, pp. 16–35.

Kiely, Bartholomew. (1982). "Consolation, Desolation and the Changing of Symbols: A Reflection on the Rules for Discernment in the Exercises." In *The Spiritual Exercises of St. Ignatius Loyola in Present-Day Application.* Rome: Centrum Ignatianum Spiritualitatis, pp. 123–56.

Kluckhohn, Clyde, and Henry A. Murray. (1948). *Personality in Nature, Society and Culture.* New York: Alfred A. Knopf.

Lonergan, Bernard. (1972). *Method in Theology.* New York: Herder and Herder.

———. (1985). "Prolegomena to the Study of the Emerging Religious Consciousness of Our Time." In Frederick E. Crowe, ed. *Third Collection.* New York: Paulist Press, pp. 55–73.

Luzbetak, Louis J. (1988). *The Church and Cultures.* Maryknoll, N. Y.: Orbis Books.

Mbiti, John S. (1969). *African Religions and Philosophy.* London: Heinemann Educational Books, Ltd.

Pobee, John S. (1979). *Toward an African Theology.* Nashville, Tenn.: Abingdon.

Ray, Benjamin. (1976). *African Religions: Symbol, Ritual and Community.* Englewood Cliffs, N.J.: Prentice-Hall, Inc.

Twesigye, Emmanuel K. (1987). *Common Ground: Christianity, African Religion and Philosophy.* New York: Peter Lang Publishing Co.

2

The Importance of Intercultural Communication Skills

MARINA HERRERA, Ph.D.

Communication is the core of any spiritual direction or counseling experience. Therefore, before presenting some recommendations that may help spiritual directors in their interactions with persons from a culture other than their own, it is imperative that we look at some of the underlying assumptions that govern all human communication.

COMMUNICATION AND CULTURE

While the dynamics of the communication process are studied and practiced in college courses everywhere, the process of intercultural communication is only recently attracting the attention it deserves as our world, and the United States in particular, becomes the arena for exchanges and collaborative projects with peoples from all over the globe. The different dynamics in intercultural communications are especially important in spiritual direction because the sincerity and the high motivation of both directors and those directed have the effect of downplaying the difficulties that can exist in these situations.

There is also a widespread belief among many highly spiritually minded people that, at their deepest levels, humans are all the same and that difficulties and misunderstandings only occur at the mundane and less perfect levels already overcome by someone who seeks spiritual direction. While there may be some truth in these beliefs, it is crucial nevertheless that spiritual directors understand that at the core level of personality there is a hidden, highly patterned level of culture that is unspoken and internalized in the normal process of socialization that we all experience as we grow into adulthood. This is the primary level culture (PLC), which is

... particularly resistant to manipulative attempts to change it from the outside. The rules may be violated or bent, but people are fully aware that something wrong has occurred. In the meantime, the rules remain intact and change according to an internal dynamic all their own. Unlike the law of religious or political dogma, these rules cannot be changed by fiat, nor can they be imposed on others against their will, because they are already internalized (Hall 1983:7).

Spiritual directors who frequently find themselves directing people from different cultures will do a great service to themselves as well as to those who seek their ministry if they become convers: ant with the growing field of intercultural communication, listen to the accounts of misunderstandings that abound in political, business, and international relief efforts, and learn from the growing body of such information.

Spiritual directors, who act within a highly specialized field of human communication, are not exempt from keeping abreast of these developments to prepare themselves to deal with the rapidly increasing numbers of peoples from every culture who still continue to find in these shores the fulfillment of long-suppressed dreams for spiritual, political, and economic freedoms.

Continued neglect of this area will inevitably lead to the continued alienation from the Catholic Church that many immigrants, especially Hispanics, are experiencing. While this neglect is mostly unintended, it is nevertheless very real. It is caused in part because the increased interest in spiritual direction has been happening among members of the majority culture, who share more homogeneous primary level cultures than those of more recent arrivals. As a result, the rules governing the communication exchanges between director and directed have been developing within a monocultural/ linguistic context with little interest in the issues pertaining to a cross-cultural situation. It is only when the spiritual director has an opportunity to go abroad or exchange ideas with directors of other cultures that curiosity in this area begins. This may lead to a desire to learn more and read a book such as this one, a mere beginning in a vastly uncharted sea of human possibilities as well as conflicts.

The other reason for this neglect is due to the fact that very often members of minority cultures in this country are not in a stable and secure socioreligious position to pursue spiritual questions that can be entertained when the more immediate human needs of the person are reasonably met. This is not to say that persons from minority cultures are not interested in spiritual issues. On the contrary, spiritual realities and how they interact and affect their lives are among the only constants enjoyed by a person in transition from another culture.

A PERSONAL ILLUSTRATION

An illustration from my own personal life will clarify this point. While many directors in this country who have discovered the rich tradition of spiritual direction in the Catholic tradition think that this is a new phenomenon taking place only here in the United States, Spanish men and women religious working with youth in Latin America have for decades been using a tradition of spiritual direction that goes back to the great mystics, especially Teresa of Avila; John of the Cross; Ignatius of Loyola, creator of the most popular tool for religious development, The Spiritual Exercises; and in more recent times, the Way of Monsignor Escrivà, founder of Opus Dei.

As early as the mid-fifties, when I was growing up in Bani, on the southern coast of the Dominican Republic and attending a school operated by the Carmelite Sisters from Spain, we were all encouraged to have a spiritual director. That role was almost always played by one of the nuns, although the Canadian Scarboro Fathers who ran the only parish in town were also available, especially to the older teenagers and adults. Through the guidance of the nuns, who were attentive listeners, we were helped to discover the vocation we were to follow in our adult life. We read the lives of the saints and were encouraged to learn the poetry of the great Carmelite mystics and to express our yearnings for God through poetry and letters — prototypes of today's journals.

The sisters were well-steeped in the spiritual teachings of their Carmelite forebears, but they also led us to admire and love the missionary zeal of Therese of Lisieux. While those experiences are now more than three decades old, the lessons of the spiritual life that I learned then have enabled me to overcome all the tribulations and withstand the successes of my adult life. They have provided my goals at different stages of my spiritual awareness and have also left an indelible mark enhancing the quality of my spiritual life, which I characterize as the link that provided continuity with my beginnings and the required constant presence for my personality to have the necessary secure base from which to explore, grow, and experiment with new ideas and possibilities.

After uprooting myself from my family and the country of my birth to pursue a mission career in this country in the early 1960s, most of the familiar elements of my youth disappeared. After a long flight from Santo Domingo through Miami, then to Detroit, and finally to Adrian, Michigan, I found myself in a place totally different in climate and texture, smells and sights from my native Bani. Where corn and snow were in great abundance and set in what seemed endless plains in my new home, my old one had a wealth of coffee beans, sugar cane, and blue waters and sky. Some readers might think this not too important in matters of the spirit. But it was crucial for me as I struggled to relate to a new culture and language, a new role and identity away from all that had defined me until then.

The absence of all familiar visual, olfactory, and tactile realities of my earliest religious awakening served to disembody, to some extent, the religious experience of my early adulthood. In their absence, other dimensions of my knowing became prominent: the memory of poetry and songs that had been deeply engrained in my being. Those became my anchor from which I was slowly able to define my missionary goals. After more than fifteen years of trying to understand, articulate, and teach people about the difficulties that mar the process of cross-cultural communication, I have found that much of my work today began in the joys and challenges of trying to relate, understand, and be understood by those significant religious persons from different cultures and in the case of the Canadian fathers, of a different language as well.

The key to my understanding of those "disembodied" religious experiences, as well as the difficulties I encountered in trying to communicate my spiritual aspirations and hopes to the sisters who oversaw my spiritual formation in the United States, did not come until almost twenty years after my arrival. This was mediated by a providential encounter with a friend who had become involved in the preparation of Peace Corps volunteers for the Caribbean. That conversation opened me up to the whole field of intercultural communication and introduced me to the many thinkers and artisans laboring to understand and facilitate the countless exchanges taking place daily within our world at every level. Through the Society for Intercultural Education, Training and Research (SIETAR) I met many dedicated people who sought to explain the numerous failures of service programs abroad such as the Peace Corps. Their field of interest includes areas such as the reasons Americans are so "tongue-tied" and cannot communicate in any language other than English and how to correct this situation; the business advances of other countries who seem to work successfully here and the failures of Americans to do the same in other countries; the many avoidable diplomatic snafus on the part of Americans, which the foreign tabloids love to highlight and the American press keeps off the front pages.

Discovering all of this was a little shocking, because it was the first indication I had that what businesses and the political establishment were doing in intercultural relations was much more significant than what Church missionaries (both at home and abroad) were doing in order to accomplish something which in my opinion deserved much better preparation. These religious persons were, for the most part, usually more altruistically motivated than the myriad experts in intercultural communication conferences but were more difficult to convince of the need for changes in approaching and understanding the questions of cross-cultural communication because the Church has, to a large extent, been operating as a multinational organization since its beginning years. The successful experiences of missionaries all over the world clouded the many failures. It still gives many the mistaken notion that when you are trying to sell "material" goods you need to know the culture of your client, but when you are trying to preach and teach the Word of God and the doctrines of your religious faith, human rules of communication do not apply.

CAUSES OF INTERCULTURAL MISUNDERSTANDING

The kernel of what I have learned about intercultural communication is found in the four seminal books of Edward Hall, the cultural anthropologist who has changed forever the way we view time, space, and culture as integral elements in human interaction. While he was not the first to observe many of the behaviors and their outcomes that he describes and analyzes, he has, perhaps more than any other contemporary observer and investigator of culture, been able to penetrate deeply into the primary level cultures, wherein lie the most serious obstacles to fruitful cross-cultural communication.[1]

All of us come out of college knowing at least one definition of culture. The problems that arise when we try to understand and explore issues of cross-cultural communication begin precisely with that fact. We think we understand that which we can define, and there is overwhelming evidence of the many ways in which we barely grasp how human beings are capable of so many different behaviors. They eat and enjoy or dislike great varieties of food, believe and act out of deep convictions born from many different religious experiences, desire for themselves so many tangibles and intangibles which are not easily systematized, fail so miserably in communicating both in their own language and in the languages of others. A recent study found that 50 percent of marriages in the United States fail and almost 90 percent of those failures can be attributed to poor communication skills between the partners. These failures are not any less for peoples of the same cultures and language than for those whose language and cultures are different.

In view of such facts and given that the science of intercultural communication is still fairly new, what can be said about communication between two persons from different cultures within the context of spiritual direction? What follows is mostly intended to explain the relationship between a director, whom we are assuming is from the dominant culture, and the directed, who is from a culture that has not been defining values and setting the rules of exchange for the others. That dominant culture, which is not necessarily a majority culture, I term a "professional" or "technical" culture. The other cultures, which may or may not be linguistically different, I call "personal" or traditional cultures.

The more I encounter people from these cultures, the more I am convinced that these characterizations help establish the commonalities and differences between the various cultures of Northern Europe and the United States (technical cultures) and the cultures of Asia, Africa, and Latin America (personal cultures). While vastly different in many of the externals of their own cultures, each of the groups shares many similarities in their cultural inner structures that allow them to establish unique bonds with each other as they relate in someone else's territory.

I recently gave a presentation to eight students from six nations of Africa who were attending a Washington-area seminary. They thought I had lived in Africa because they felt I spoke to their experiences and problems in trying to understand American culture and the seminary culture in particular. I have never been to Africa, but I have been deeply touched by the experiences of many descendants of Africans in my country as well as here. I have always found many converging strands in our approach to life and relationships.

The second biggest culprit bringing failure in cross-cultural communication seems to lie in the fact that while we say we acknowledge differences in cultures, we continue to be angered, express disbelief, and fail to understand when someone responds in ways that are different from our own responses. We have a strong urge to project unto others the same motivations we have, to expect from others the identical responses we would give, or to pursue answers and goals reached through the same logic and reasoning we use. This tendency, which cultural anthropologists call "projected cognitive similarity," makes us define the other in terms of our particular structure of reality, which may or may not have considered the value or significance of the others. In such instances the possibility of a fruitful exchange between those two persons diminishes considerably.

Thirdly, in order to enter the field of cross-cultural direction with some sense of success, we must give up three deeply cherished understandings regarding communication: 1) that language alone is the main carrier of communication; 2) that printed language is more important for the communication process than oral, tactile, or nontext-oriented visuals; and 3) that nonverbal language is the same across cultures (a belief clung to even where differences in linguistic expressions are accepted and recognized).

The first fallacy leads us to believe that the biggest misunderstandings take place between people who speak different languages. However, every day we experience misunderstandings between people of the same linguistic family, for example, partners in marriage. Sometimes the United States Senate or House of Representatives may debate a bill for years before it is passed. The reasons for the delayed passage are not a lack of a common language but rather that this language is a tool for views and goals which are not shared in common. When those goals are opposed to one's plans or expectations, it does not matter how well you communicate the message, because it will not be received; if it is received, it will not change certain positions and therefore no joint solution can be found. This is best exemplified in the debate over abortion, in which both sides have the finest speakers yet are becoming increasingly recalcitrant in their views.

Because of our great access to books, newspapers, and billboards, we feel that anyone who cannot read is not fully a human being. In fact, the way in which the society labels those who are not capable or not interested in reading is as unenlightened and biased in favor of the literate as we have been in the recent past with the use of pejorative terms for persons with physical disabilities. We have assumed that integrity and truth are the characteristics of the literate and that dishonesty and incompetence describe the "illiterate." While it is true that we who are print-oriented get our clues from printed words, others get theirs in other ways. I will never forget the experience of knowing two women in New York. One had a Ph.D. in philosophy but feared the subways because she was never sure she was following the signs correctly. The other, who could barely sign her name and did household chores for people in all the boroughs, was able to find her way around the entire subway system without batting an eye. Her English was also quite limited, but neither of these shortcomings stopped her from accomplishing her goal of earning enough money to sustain herself and her family who still lived outside the United States. To accomplish that goal she needed great mobility.

Finally, while we know that persons who speak different languages will have strained communications, if the person receiving spiritual direction is able to communicate in English quite well, even if she or he is from a different linguistic family, our tendency is to interpret the nonverbal aspects of the person's communication in the same way we interpret similar aspects of our own. We have no trouble saying that we do not understand something that is said in poor English, but it is unlikely that we would ask a person of Hispanic extraction capable of speaking English why she speaks so loud. We interpret her loudness using the same measures for interpreting voice volume that we use with people from our own culture. This tendency to assume that nonverbal communications are universal is perhaps at the heart of most major communication breakdowns.

IMPORTANCE OF THE NONVERBAL

The communication process is thought to be mostly nonverbal: Some cultural anthropologists and sociolinguists suggest that 90 percent of exchanges are in this category. Contrary to what most people think, the most important of these nonverbal clues are not visual ones, but auditory indicators such as tone, speed, and emphasis. Speed and tone are baffling because these tacit elements of communication seem for the most part to be outside our conscious control and therefore cannot be changed at will, in contrast to the words we use.

For example, chronemics is a nonverbal element of communication that determines the speed with which we respond to the person who addresses us. While some assume that the accepted rule is "I finish and you begin after a very brief pause," the Hispanic responds on the counterpoint beat. I barely have the last syllable out of my mouth when the other person is ready to begin, particularly if one is deeply engaged with the speaker. This is considered rude by those whose sense of propriety demands that you do not start until I have finished. Other groups, such as Native Americans, prefer to pause for a while, sometimes in ways that exasperate the speaker and cause tensions in the relationship.

Similar observations can be made about space, positions for demonstrating interest, clues to let the speaker know that we are listening and with them, positions of those in authority vs. those with less power, the non-threatening and nonsexual use of touch on the part of the speaker as a gentle way to draw the listener back into the conversation. This is especially evident among those cultures where eye contact is more subtle and less aggressive than in the United States.

CONCLUSION: FOCUSING ON PERSONS

It is not culture per se to which one must adapt, but culture as manifested and encountered in the behavior of individuals of the other culture. Therefore, when we consider spiritual direction between persons of different cultures, some simple rules may facilitate the process, but these must also be accompanied by a study of the lessons involved in these exchanges and a firm grasp of the ways in which primary level culture affects our exchanges.

The motivation or sincere desire to understand, appreciate, and exchange with the other is the key element in communication between and across cultures. This motivation can have a spiritual basis but it also can be self-interested in a positive sense. We anticipate personal benefits, enrichment, and the expansion of our own awareness of the limitless creativity of God in the variety of creatures we encounter. "My enemy's army is for aggression but mine is only for defense."

Negative emotional reactions to a pattern of behavior we are not used to must be kept carefully in check when we are dealing with a person from a different culture. A time for withholding judgment on the person's behavior is absolutely needed in these situations. There are ample reasons to indicate that behavior that is not understood is always labeled as negative or destructive. "Chinese people cannot be too intelligent when they continue to offer food to their ancestors even when they know the dead cannot eat. Can Westerners be very clever when they keep placing flowers at the tombs of their dead when they know the dead cannot see them or smell them?"

Cross-cultural communication requires of us an examination of our own cultural presuppositions, especially in regard to the rightness or wrongness of specific behavior or behavior that is simply "different."

NOTES

1. Hall's books are the following: *The Silent Language* (Garden City, N.Y.: Anchor Press, 1963), a classical study of communication, especially its nonverbal dimension, as it is affected by culture; *The Hidden Dimension* (Garden City, N.Y.:

Doubleday & Co., Inc., 1966), the significance of social and personal space and people's perception of it in relation to cross-cultural exchanges; *Beyond Culture* (Garden City, N.Y.: Anchor Press, 1976), a proposal for a global shift toward "cultural literacy" that will enable the human race to escape the constraints of "covert culture," those aspects of culture taken for granted; *The Dance of Life: The Other Dimension of Time* (New York: Anchor Books, 1983), shows how time is an organizer of activities, a synthesizer and integrator, and a special language that reveals how we really feel about each other.

3

Predispositions for Dialogue in Spiritual Direction

DOMINIC MARUCA, SJ

As we enter the last decade of our millennium, the Church in which we are living clearly has become multicultural.[1] Throughout the world there is a growing awareness of the cultural pluralism of humanity. Long before the term *inculturation* was coined by cultural anthropologists,[2] missionaries had been adapting themselves to the local cultural settings in which they found themselves and appropriating elements which did not compromise the Church's basic faith in Christ. But in the wake of Vatican II's teaching,[3] theologians have been stressing that the new challenge we are facing is precisely that of meeting other cultures in a spirit of honest and humble dialogue, as regional churches begin to mutually criticize and enrich one another. We are being encouraged to reflect on the theological issues at stake and to devise a new pastoral approach adequate to the problems accompanying this new development.[4]

The aim of this essay is to consider how this new and growing challenge is affecting spiritual direction. More than ever, directors are being invited abroad not only to minister to seminaries from different regions but also to conduct workshops for priests and religious and to collaborate with a broad range of laypersons in a variety of ways.

There is a similar flow in the opposite direction: More and more persons are crossing national and international boundaries, some to engage in studies, others finding themselves displaced or forced to emigrate for political, economic, or social reasons. They, too, seek spiritual directors who are sensitive to their distinctive cultural heritage. One religious formator described how he felt about his situation in these terms: "I am standing on a middle ground and looking two ways: toward the congregation that has

33

missioned me to initiate new members into the order, and towards people of a different culture, whom I am missioned to serve."[5]

Clearly, we are at a critical point. We can take advantage of this new opportunity or allow it to be added to the distressing list of past failures.

> The experiences of our history make us painfully aware of the fact that not all contact between different cultures means automatically an enrichment for the cultures concerned. Culture-contact can also be destructive . . . Every one-directional process of cultural assimilation ignores the riches of originality and creativity in a given culture and leads to an impoverishment of human values. A fruitful communication between cultures has to take on the form of a dialogue . . . Through dialogue one not only learns to understand the other, but acquires also a deeper understanding of oneself.[6]

The question before us is this: Can we directors prepare ourselves to meet this new opportunity by learning how to engage respectfully in dialogue with persons of various cultures? It is difficult to become conscious of something so elusive as the implicit suppositions underlying our manner of dealing with persons of different cultures. I must confess that I first became aware of my deficient mind-set only indirectly as I came to recognize that my style of engaging in dialogue was counterproductive. My capacity for listening attentively, resisting the urge to confront prematurely, and responding in a more tentative manner was not what it could and should have been. By reflecting on three basic principles that have been acknowledged as axiomatic in spiritual direction for many centuries, I discovered that I was failing to observe them, especially in cross-cultural situations. Underlying this failure were certain unacknowledged prejudices or presuppositions on my part. (Need I mention that a greater sensitivity to the demands of cross-cultural situations improved my mode of dealing with persons within my own culture?)

The three closely related principles that enabled me to acknowledge my latent biases were these: 1) Each person who comes to us for spiritual direction should be recognized and respected as unique. 2) But uniqueness does not mean self-sufficiency; each of us labors under the common human tendency to overlook our own defects and limitations, therefore we all need supplementary instruction and correction. 3) The more sacred and sublime a truth is, the greater is the need to impart it gradually and to adapt it to each person's temperament and stage of development. Let's reflect on these principles more leisurely and in greater depth. Since a change in perspective is usually the prerequisite for achieving a more global vision, it may be that by becoming aware of the presuppositions with which many persons of diverse cultural backgrounds commonly approach one another, we will broaden our horizon and enhance our capacity to dialogue with others.

RESPECTING THE UNIQUENESS OF EACH PERSON

Experienced directors are unanimous in teaching that one's own spiritual itinerary is not to be made normative for others. Saint Therese of the Child

Jesus, in her role as Mistress of Novices, noted that all souls have practically the same battles to wage but each has to do so in her own way. She tells us that she became conscious of an obligation to forget her own tastes, her own personal conceptions so that she could guide souls not along the road that she herself had traversed but along the particular path which Jesus was pointing out to them. She recognized that she had to refrain from trying to conduct all novices in the same way.[7]

Similarly, Saint Ignatius Loyola, in all his activity as a director, maintained a delicate balance: He appeared above all as one faithful in transmitting the message that he had received from God in the graces of his mystical life, namely, the message to promote a spirituality of service through love. But at the same time he was very independent of his own interior ways, careful to direct each person according to the ways marked out by God for the individual, docile to the lessons of experience. He was penetrating and quick to discern and then bring to accomplishment at any cost the chief desires of God with respect to each person, taking into account all the differences by which each was distinguished.[8]

Why this reverential respect for the uniqueness of each person? It is not simply to assure psychological effectiveness. There are more radical doctrinal and theological reasons, the first of which is the freedom of God reflected in each human person. This freedom is manifested and must be respected continuously by insisting on what is called the primacy of grace: its absolute gratuity and utterly personal character. As a corollary to this truth we must recognize that there is simply no way in which any human director can specify in advance exactly which path God will choose to lead any given person to the holiness and perfection of love to which he or she is being called. Let's consider this concretely.

So much depends on an incalculable number of variables: hereditary factors and family background; religious training or lack thereof; traumas during childhood or adolescence; sinful patterns of behavior; experience of moral, religious, and intellectual conversion; training in prayer and penance; the experience of love and affection or conversely that of neglect, oppression, and injustice. The list could be extended indefinitely. To ignore the distinctiveness of each person seeking guidance and direction is to disregard the handiwork of the Creator, who knows and loves each creature infinitely more than any human director ever can know and love them!

The first obligation of any director is to respect this truth and keep it ever in mind. His or her primary contribution is to direct the attention of each person to the Spirit of God present and operative within each of us; to help him or her recognize, appreciate, and embrace the movements of that Spirit. It is not to impose our views, our values, our judgments. This principle is recognized by spiritual masters as basic and absolutely inviolable.

As we now shift our focus specifically to the cross-cultural level, we may ask ourselves: How well have we been observing this principle in our deal-

ings as spiritual directors with persons from a cultural background totally
or partially different from our own?

I learned somewhat to my embarrassment that I shared the natural pref-
erence people seem to have for their own nation and culture. C. S. Lewis
relates a humorous story to illustrate what he calls a firm, even prosaic
belief that one's own nation, in sober fact, has long been and still is mark-
edly superior to all others.

> I once ventured to say to an old clergyman who was voicing this sort of
> patriotism, "But, sir, aren't we told that every people thinks its own men are
> the bravest and its own women the fairest in the world?" He replied with
> total gravity—he could not have been graver if he had been saying the Creed
> at the altar—"Yes, but in England it's true." Lewis concludes with the obser-
> vation: "To be sure, this conviction had not made my friend (God rest his
> soul) a villain; only an extremely lovable old ass. It can however produce asses
> that kick and bite."[9]

What I had to admit was that at times I was making my cultural background and values normative for others. Proof? Honest dialogue had
become impossible. Persons coming to me for spiritual direction had
already benefited from a social, intellectual, and religious formation proper
to their own culture. Certain values and patterns of behavior that had been
transmitted to them enjoyed an integrity and beauty of their own. I came
to recognize that failure on my part to acknowledge this truth by an attempt
to impose a system of formation and direction totally alien to those inher-
ited acquired values and characteristics not only made any dialogue impossible but also constituted a gross injustice against my neighbor and
irreverence toward our Creator.

The most direct way to learn how I could be of service to any particular
person was, of course, simply to listen. By listening a director receives the
material that constitutes the elements for direction; for example, what
images the person has of God, of the world, of the human person. One's
particular understanding of the Church and its mission to the world, of
one's personal vocation, of one's values and vision also can come into sharp
focus.

To sum up this first point: An expression of our respect and love for the
people of any nation is our willingness to learn their language and literature, to grow in appreciation of their art forms and symbols, their history,
geography, economic and political structure. Within this awareness of the
beauty and integrity of the other person's culture, we become better dis-
posed to listening attentively to what they wish to tell us about themselves;
consequently, we become more capable of directing them wisely. This is
not to imply that spiritual directors must totally set aside all the experience
they have derived from their own training and culture. The second spiritual
axiom to be considered will discuss how we can draw on that experience
and training most effectively and respectfully.

OPENNESS AND RECIPROCITY IN CHALLENGING, INSTRUCTING, BEING CORRECTED

This second principle is a correlative to the first. I used to presume that persons coming for direction recognized that they had at best only a limited understanding of the ways in which God deals with humankind. I thought that they were coming with a willingness to be instructed, challenged, and corrected if necessary. After all, a distinctive characteristic of the Catholic tradition of spiritual direction is an eagerness to profit from the rich heritage of the experiential wisdom of the past and from the variety of peoples embodying the Mystery of Christ today. Those who prefer to enclose themselves in private experience run the risk of being cut off from the vast reservoir of past wisdom and from the fresh streams of contemporary development.[10]

In working in cross-cultural settings, I've learned to question those naive assumptions and to make my expectations more realistic. I now think that most persons who come for spiritual direction come with the common desire to be accepted and understood, with a hope that they will be loved for who they are, as they are. Many are so easily intimidated by any confrontation that is ill-advised or premature. Gradually they will acknowledge that they are in need of guidance and correction. But silence and a smile may be the prelude to being welcomed into their hearts. Like the Lord himself, we must stand at the door, knock, and then wait patiently for the invitation to enter (Rev. 3:20).

This reverential restraint and reticence can become a source of tension if not properly understood. Spiritual directors are in a sense an embodiment of the Tradition that they represent and have a responsibility to present that Tradition clearly and comprehensively.[11] When and how to present our Tradition calls for delicate discernment. By way of illustration, let's consider one area in which we are bound to make known our Christian Tradition, that of prayer. Dialogue can promote, I submit, both an enriched mutual understanding as well as protection from certain errors.

In its letter on "Some Aspects of Christian Meditation," dated October 15, 1989,[12] the Congregation for the Doctrine of the Faith provides us with authoritative teaching on Christian prayer. A number of passages in this letter strike me as potential "talking points" with persons coming for spiritual direction. Let us consider a few of them. It may be that the substance of what is being taught is solidly grounded, but the manner of expressing it may evoke questions in the minds of persons with other cultural backgrounds.

The occasion for the letter was pastoral solicitude concerning the interest awakened in forms of meditation associated with some Eastern religions. The letter asks whether these different styles and methods can enrich our heritage and, if so, what are the criteria of a doctrinal and pastoral character that might allow spiritual directors to instruct others in these new forms of prayer while remaining faithful to the truth revealed in Jesus? I interpret this as a mandate to engage in dialogue with those from other traditions. By way of introduction we are reminded that any discussion on prayer must start with a certain premise: Christian prayer is always determined by the structure of our faith, namely, that God is God and creatures are creatures. Prayer then can be defined as "a personal, intimate and profound dialogue between a human person and God" (n. 3). This is an excellent starting point for dialogue.

The first section is a fine exposition of "Christian Prayer in the Light of Revelation." It highlights the Bible as the primary teacher of how to pray (nn. 4–5); then it draws on the teaching of Vatican II (*Dei Verbum*, nn. 2, 3, 5, 8, 21, 25) to describe prayer as a dialogue between God and God's friends that enables us to discover the deep meaning of Sacred Scripture in both an ecclesial setting and in a personal manner (nn. 6–7). Once again I think this is a solid introduction for persons coming to us to be instructed on the nature of Christian prayer.

The next section is entitled, "Erroneous Ways of Praying." The letter draws upon the long history of the Church, reaching back to the early centuries, to caution us against incorrect forms of prayer that have continued to reappear throughout history. It singles out two fundamental deviations. 1) Pseudo-gnosticism: the notion that matter is something impure and degraded, imprisoning the soul in an ignorance from which prayer must free it and raise it to a pure state of superior knowledge. Those who achieve such a spiritual state can dispense with Christian faith as something superfluous, proper only to simple believers. 2) Messalianism: by identifying the grace of the Holy Spirit with the psychological experience of God's presence in the soul, this teaching denies that we are united to God always in a mysterious way, for example, by way of the sacraments of the Church. Moreover, this teaching fails to recognize that union with God can be achieved through experiences of affliction and desolation, and not just during times of euphoric emotion. The letter cautions us, moreover, against any effort to overcome the distance that always will separate creature from Creator, as though there ought not to be such a distance; it teaches that we must beware of considering the way Christ walked on earth, and by which he wishes to lead us to the Father, as a way that has been surpassed; it wants to guard us against bringing down to the level of natural psychology what has been regarded as pure grace.

These errors have reappeared in history and continue to be an appealing "quick way" of finding God. They tend to disregard the human-earthly dimension of life. I found much in this section which has served as points of departure for honest dialogue. Similarly in the following sections on the "Christian Way to Union with God" (nn. 13–15), "Questions of Method" (nn. 16–25), "Psychological-Corporal Methods" (nn. 26–28) and "I Am the Way" (nn. 29–31), there is much material for discussion.

To sum up this section, it seems to me that two balancing dispositions are desirable in our dialoguing about prayer: 1) a deep conviction of the value of our own spiritual Tradition so that we can present it courageously; and 2) an awareness of its possible limitations such as to assure respect for other approaches. For example, at one time I presumed that our abstract manner of conceiving and expressing a reality is superior to that of more "primitive" peoples. Martin Buber made me aware of this mind-set with a striking question: Should distance be expressed in terms of a measurable quantity or in terms of relationships? We Westerners say "far away" to describe distance; the Zulu has a sentence-word instead that means: "where one cries 'mother I am lost.' "[13] By what criteria do we presume that the abstract mode of speaking is superior to the concrete world of human relationships? Is the concrete and particular necessarily more "primitive" than the abstract and universal, especially in the area of prayerful union with God?[14]

GRADUAL PRESENTATION AND ADAPTATION OF GENERAL PRINCIPLES

The third and final principle for our consideration is how we are to present the truths of our faith. There are certain formal spiritual and moral principles that are considered to be generally if not universally valid, such as the need for self-denial as a condition for following Christ; a detachment from material things; purity of mind and heart; universal love, especially of one's enemies. Concern to impart these principles in all their integrity can lead us to strive for a premature clarity to the detriment of human relationships, to exercise a brutal honesty at the expense of Christ-like compassion. I have found this matter one that calls for delicate, prayerful discernment and consultation with others more knowledgeable about a given culture. How are certain principles to be held firmly while being adapted to the pace of growth and development of the persons we are seeking to evangelize?

John Henry Cardinal Newman helped me on this point. He noted that in the early Church a principle of "economy" was observed in preaching, instructing, and catechizing with respect to the divine ordinances and the duties of Christians.

As Almighty God did not all at once introduce the Gospel to the world, and thereby gradually prepared men for its profitable reception, so, according to the doctrine of the early Church, it was a duty, for the sake of the heathen among whom they lived, to observe a great reserve and caution in communicating to them the knowledge of "the whole counsel of God." This cautious dispensation of the truth, after the manner of a discreet and vigilant steward, is denoted by the word "economy." It is a mode of acting which comes under the head of Prudence, one of the four Cardinal Virtues. The Principle of the

Economy is this: that out of various courses, in religious conduct or statement, all and each allowable antecedently and in themselves, that ought to be taken which is most expedient and most suitable at the time for the object in hand.[15]

He goes on to give instances of its application and exercise in Scripture, where we see that Divine Providence gradually imparted to the world in general and to the Jews in particular the knowledge of God's will. Cardinal Newman concludes that this rule is to be applied in dealings between peoples of different religious, political, or social views.

Spiritual teachers have practiced and recommended this same principle in the spiritual direction of anyone who wishes to scale the heights of Christian perfection. The pace at which persons advance is not a fixed one, nor do they proceed in a lock-step formation. As we discussed earlier in this essay, God's grace cannot be programmed mechanically. The measure and intensity of God's gifts depends on many factors: the nature and generosity of each person, mental or spiritual capacity, age, physical strength, degree of education, moral and spiritual dispositions, good will and earnest desires, the special purpose for which a person comes for spiritual direction, acceptance of the evangelical counsels. Premature exposition of spiritual ideals, indiscriminate exhortations to diligence and zeal, excessive warnings and admonitions about problems and dangers can lead to debilitating anxiety, frustration, discouragement. Patience and prudence are therefore absolutely necessary.

What is prescribed on the individual level, I submit, is even more crucial on the cross-cultural level. Cultural anthropologists warn us that "The split of the contemporary post-colonial conscience between Christianity and Western civilization nurtures the dreadful illusion that it is possible to isolate Christianity in its essence"[16] by divesting it of the foreign elements borrowed from Western culture. At the risk of appearing facetious, I would express this misperception by observing that Christianity is not like the formula for Coca-Cola, which can be exported to diverse lands, mixed with local water, and distributed for consumption. Discretion is called for as we seek to share the wisdom of the ages with persons being evangelized and guided to the fullness of perfect love. In a far-ranging, perceptive essay entitled, "The Church, Society and Politics,"[17] Avery Dulles reminds us that each culture has a distinctive attitude toward life and death, wealth and poverty, power and weakness, truth and falsehood, pleasure and pain. In formulating specific approaches, the movement from principle to practice is complex and delicate. In a similar manner, it seems to me that the spiritual director has a formidable challenge in speaking of spiritual principles and their practice. Our capacity to speak a healing and transforming word to those who come to us will depend on our sensitivity as well as our honesty and courage. This is not a question of whether we will compromise our principles, but one of flexibility and discretion in applying them.

CONCLUSION

Spiritual direction can be viewed as an exercise in the asceticism of truth and love demanded by the very nature of genuine dialogue. To listen attentively to other persons, respecting their uniqueness and not imposing our own agenda; to challenge and confront others patiently and progressively, without frightening them or fearing their disapproval; to proceed gradually in communicating truths founded unshakably in our faith—these are all expressions of love for our neighbor and reverence for the truth. Such honest, humble dialogue demands faith and freedom on the part of everyone engaged therein. My thesis in brief has been this: Any attitude that impedes or precludes the possibility of dialogue with persons who come to us for spiritual direction diminishes our effectiveness as spiritual directors. This is true in every situation, but especially in a cross-cultural setting. We have reflected on three such crucial attitudes or predispositions: 1) any feeling, conscious or unconscious, of ethnocentric superiority that prevents us from respecting the uniqueness of each person who comes to us; 2) failure to recognize the need to confront and challenge others with utmost caution and humility, as well as with courage and honesty; 3) unwillingness to wait patiently for divine grace to prepare and dispose each person for the full truth of our Christian faith.

I find an excellent model to follow in our Risen Lord's manner of dealing with the two disciples walking along the way to Emmaus (Luke 24:13–35). They were disillusioned and dejected; their hearts were downcast because their hopes had been shattered. Jesus emerged from the shadows and fell into step with them. The Divine Physician lanced the festering wound of their depression and let it drain through self-expression; he simply asked a question and listened attentively. After this attentive hearing he confronted them firmly but gently, berating them for their lack of faith in God's full message; then, step-by-step, he illuminated the mystery of redemptive suffering as their hearts became capable of embracing it. He respected their freedom, awaited their invitation to stay with them, and finally led them to the recognition of his identity in the mysterious presence of the bread he broke with them. In brief, he respected their limited horizon and the pain of their personal experience, broadened that horizon, and supplemented their inadequate understanding, gradually leading them to a fuller appreciation of the mystery of God. In this way he inspired them to return to Jerusalem, to the Church, where they could share and make their story part of the greater story, being confirmed in their faith through the experience of others.

The ultimate secret of successful spiritual direction, as of all things in our distinct cultural settings, is the secret of love. Christian love, as St. Paul has reminded us, is "always patient and kind; it is never jealous; love is never boastful or conceited; it is never rude or selfish; it does not take offense, and is not resentful. Love takes no pleasure in other people's sins but delights in the truth; it is always ready to excuse, to trust, to hope, and to endure whatever comes" (1 Cor. 13:4–7).

NOTES

1. "Borders Open; Barriers Still Stand," Address of John Paul II to the participants in the Plenary Session of the Pontifical Council for Culture, *L'Osservatore Romano* (January 12, 1990).

2. Ary Roest Crollius, SJ, and Théoneste Nkéramihigo, SJ, *What Is So New About Inculturation?* (Rome: Gregorian Press, 1984), p. 5.

3. E.g., *Gaudium et Spes* 42; *Ad Gentes* 10, 19.

4. Avery Dulles, *The Reshaping of Catholicism: Current Challenges in the Theology of the Church* (New York: Harper & Row, 1988), pp. 34–37. The Catholic Theological Society of America chose "Inculturation and Catholicity" as its theme for its 1990 annual convention. *See* the *Proceedings of the Forty-Fifth Annual Convention*, vol. 45 (San Francisco, June 6–9, 1990).

5. Martin O'Reilly, CFC, "Cross-Cultural Religious Formation," *Human Development* 11 (Spring 1990): 34.

6. Crollius and Nkéramihigo, pp. 49, 50, 52.

7. *Conseils et souvenirs* (Lisieux, 1952), pp. 6–7. Ronald Knox, in his own felicitous way, renders this passage as follows: "When you look at it from a distance, it all seems plain sailing; what's the difficulty about doing good to souls, making them love God better—in a word, turning them out on your own pattern, according to your own ideas? But when you look at it from close to, it's not plain sailing at all, nothing of the kind. You discover that trying to do good to people without God's help is no easier than making the sun shine at midnight. You discover that you've got to abandon all your own preferences, your own bright ideas, and guide souls along the road our Lord has marked out for them; you mustn't dragoon them into some path of your own choosing." *Autobiography of a Saint* (London: Harvill, 1958), p. 284.

8. Joseph de Guibert, *The Jesuits: Their Spiritual Doctrine and Practice*, tr. William J. Young, SJ (Chicago: Loyola University, 1964), pp. 107–8. He had very broad points of view so as never to look upon them as isolated individuals, but rather as persons within the whole assembly of the Church's life. Very realistic, he never confused mere means with the true end, the accessory with the essential.

9. *The Four Loves* (New York: Harcourt, Brace & World, 1960), pp. 44–45.

10. "Human groups, in the pursuit even of the highest spiritual values, are always exposed to the danger of 'individualistic' assertion of these values while excluding the rights of other persons (as can be seen in the totalitarian imposition of a state-ideology, or in various forms of religious wars) . . . Individual sociality is that aspect of human social life which expresses the need of the individual human being to be assisted by others in the realisation of his ends. This sociality is primarily receptive. Personal sociality is that aspect of human social life which results from the free self-communication of the spirit, insofar as the person realises its perfection in sharing it with other persons. This sociality is primarily communicative." Crollius and Nkéramihigo, pp. 42–43.

11. Tradition, Avery Dulles reminds us, gives continuity with the lived reality of

the past and serves as a catalyst for the future. It is not confining or retrogressive but broadens our vision and empowers us with new vision so that we can see and value what the Community sees and values. Dulles, pp. 82–87.

12. *Origins* 19 (December 28, 1989): 492–98. This letter did not intend directly to discuss different methods of prayer and meditation proper to non-Christian cultures or deal with the question of their psychological or therapeutic value; it professes to deal only with theological and spiritual implications of those methods. The footnotes in themselves constitute a rich anthology of the history of writings on Christian prayer. The commentaries which appeared in *L'Osservatore Romano,* December 20, 1989–January 20, 1990, represent the scientific research of many outstanding contemporary experts on prayer. Cf. *La Civilta Cattolica* (3 marzo 1990): 317–27; (17 marzo 1990): 521–32; (7 aprile 1990): 3–15.

13. Martin Buber, *I and Thou,* tr. Walter Kaufmann (New York: Scribners', 1970), pp. 69–70.

14. Crollius and Nkéramihigo, p. 51. Note that the origin of the attitude called "ethnocentric" is the "naive evolutionistic conception according to which all cultures are bound to develop in conformity with the model of occidental culture."

15. *Apologia Pro Vita Sua* (London: Longmans, 1892), n. F, p. 343. Cardinal Newman first proposed this principle in his work on the Arians. He defended it by drawing on the teaching of our Lord himself, that of St. Paul, the catechetical system practiced in the early Church, and the *disciplina arcani.*

16. Crollius and Nkéramihigo, p. 25.

17. Dulles, pp. 154–83.

4

Toward Integral Spirituality:
Embodiment, Ecology, and Experience of God

ANTHONY J. GITTINS, CSSp

THEMES AND VARIATIONS

Asked what he would do if he knew that the world would end on the morrow, Martin Luther unhesitatingly replied, "I would plant a tree in my garden." Each word contributes to a meditative starting point for our theme; cumulatively they express a way of being in the world with God that might be called an "ecological spirituality."[1]

Spirituality is not vacuum-packed but actualized, experienced, discovered in particular circumstances and places. A person's spirituality is not entirely private but has social ramifications. Consequently we might speak of a microspirituality and of a macrospirituality, depending on whether personal or communal aspects are emphasized. But spirituality is also inseparable from self, and since people are incarnated or embodied in unique and changing forms, we are led to a number of further questions. How variously do different people experience their embodiment? What are the effects of such experience on interpersonal relationships or relations with the wider world? What are some of the different forms of microspirituality, and how do they relate to macrospirituality? And could one suggest, tentatively and impressionistically, some correlation between types of spiritual experience and the external environment, between the microcosm of the body and the macrocosm of the universe, between a way of being on the earth and a way of experiencing God?[2]

Evidently, the human species encompasses a wide range of racial and cultural variation: Kanghiryuatjiagmiut Eskimos and Bidjandjadjara Aborigines are as different as their names, and blond Scandinavians stand in

44

striking contrast to ebony Nubians. But differences in "spirituality" are also evident if we compare the control of a saffron-robed Buddhist monk from Kampuchea, the abandon of a traditional Dogon healer from Mali, and the controlled abandon of a Sufi "whirling" dervish from Iraq.

The variation hardly ends there, since the earth itself is not presented to humanity in a single articulation but is experienced variously through many different environments or bioregions. We might say that the earth is "revealed" to people, a refraction of a multifaceted whole, both as home and as story. We make our home on its deserts and arctic wildernesses, within its temperate and tropical climates, in its highlands and valleys, forests and savannahs, islands and mainlands, caves and swamps; and we learn the story, the wisdom gleaned about the earth and beyond, about ourselves and within, and transmitted by our different communities, in revelation within a tradition or by means of religious faith and experience.

Yet there are as many kinds of homes as there are stories. Are such homes and stories, bioregions or ecologies, merely interesting variations across the earth and among people, or are they critical to its functioning and our own? If we can learn much from a consideration of the earth as a living ecosystem comprised of interrelated and significant microsystems within the macrosystem, can we learn as much from contemplation of humanity as a macrosystem united by shared consciousness and comprised of the delicate microsystems of myriad ways of being in the world?

SOCIAL STRUCTURE AND BODILY CONTROL

The question becomes much more immediate if we consider in tandem both the place in the universe and the way of being in the world of real people. In the controlled environment of a stereotypical contemplative monastery, one might experience God primarily through senses attuned to a fairly fixed world and in images selected, perhaps unconsciously, for their assumed potential to consolidate one's "spirituality." But in a world of television and airplanes, where the exotic and unusual can be as easily experienced as read about, where an active apostolic life exposes one to previously undreamed-of realities and does not spare those of delicate sensibility or modest demeanor, experience of God may be not so much in the still small voice or the blossom of an apple orchard as in the encounters of an oriental bazaar or on the palm-fringed beach, ankle-mired in the mud of a "favela" or axle-bogged in a jungle swamp.

And so what? A church concerned with purity and pollution, salvation and damnation, boundaries and margins, is as likely to emphasize values of continence and control, as a society obsessed with hedonism and power, license and freedom, experimentation and nihilism might tolerate promiscuity and spontaneity. This should not be surprising; but the assertion that the human body is always treated as an image of society, might be.[3]

Of course the body does not only find expression in extremes of absti-

nence or indulgence; there are other forms of discipline or relaxation. But
the hypothesis here is not that people individually decide on cultivated
propriety or wild abandon but that the social universe operates on people
in society to provide possibilities and limitations; a tightly organized social
universe will give rise to strong emphasis on its members' bodily control,
while a more loosely articulated society will produce opportunities for more
relaxed forms of embodiment.

But whence derived the different social universes that decorate the
earth, if not, at least in part, from creative responses to different physical
locations, congenial and hostile, bounded or open, isolated or populous?
By identifying various bioregions we should be able to see some correlation
between them and different social worlds, just as by noting the latter we
may underline some correlations between them and degrees of bodily control. In West Africa, the Mende people live in a relatively enclosed world
amid forest or woodland, rarely see the horizon, and occupy permanent
dwellings aggregated in villages separated by several miles of the land they
farm. Unostentatious, they are as self-possessed as they are proprietorial,
concerned about controlling the many spirits that populate their villages.
In East Africa, the highland Masai people live in the very open world of
unwooded rolling hills offering spectacular views of the horizon. Theirs are
rather impermanent dwellings in hamlets of only a few families, and they
are traditionally nomadic. Outgoing, highly adorned, and unhurried, they
sense the presence of the supreme being, gently brooding over their lives.

Or contrast the Bushmen of the Kalahari desert with Mbuti Pygmies of
the Ituri forest. The former are individualistic, prone to pursuing personal
vision quests, and commonly experiencing states of trance. They are also
marked by high anxiety. Not so the very social pygmies in their forest
enclaves. Their rituals are communal and they distrust personal trance
states or possession. Their lives are characterized by joyousness. Such ways
of being in the world are not whimsical but related to the very world in
which Bushmen and Pygmies actually live. And we could continue, com-
paring Sherpas in the Himalayas with Trobrianders of the Pacific Islands,
or anti-establishment, trendsetting, free-spirited, commune-living "hippies"
of the "swinging sixties," characterized by lusty physicality and altered
states of consciousness, with orthodox, traditional, disciplined, community-
living religious of the decidedly "unswinging sixties," characterized by
refined spirituality and controlled contemplation. These different social
groups lived contemporaneously on the same planet, but literally worlds
apart.[4]

Again, is it accidental or entirely a matter of personal freedom that some
people practice institutionalized female circumcision while others decorate
and display their bodies, or that some mutilate felons while other repeal
the death penalty? Is it by chance that a post-Vatican II Church, in its
uneasy move from being "always and everywhere the same" to becoming a
community of inculturated communities, should be beset with issues of

authority and service, conformity and experimentation, universality and localization, or of the ways these are manifest, such as celibacy, divorce, in-vitro fertilization, clinical abortion, and the rest? Whatever choices and tensions appear among peoples are not unrelated to their respective social structures, social organizations, and social environments.

A strong microcosm,[5] whether maintained by control of individual bodily boundaries or orifices[6] and associated fluids, or by segregation from the world outside, will produce a spirituality characterized by control, of which disdain or denial are forms. It may be manifest in control of self or others, of emotional and other responses and range, and of the environment. This marks the macrocosm as irrelevant, remote, and unrelated to the world within. Such a spirituality unrepentantly debases the macrocosm. God is domesticated, revelation is privatized, and religion is about techniques and rules.

A weak microcosm, in terms of openness to the macrocosm, is effected through release or surrender of some bodily controls,[7] boundaries, and rules, and a sensitivity to the challenges and surprises from outside. It will produce a spirituality characterized by trust and responsibility, flexibility and reciprocity, vulnerability and nurturing of self, others, and the earth. It will undertake responsibility toward the macrocosm and a stance of a learner rather than a teacher, a servant rather than a dominator. God will be not so much distant as universal, cosmic, a God of all. God's transcendence will be respected, and theology will not be narrow, doctrinaire, or partisan.

Such is the theory; in fact, across cultures and traditions, there may be considerable confusion and ambiguity. But this will still produce its fruits: social uncertainty can be expected to yield bodily and sexual ambivalence, anxiety, and experimentation.[8]

TOWARD AN ECOLOGICAL SPIRITUALITY

We can now ponder personal responses as we seek to understand behavior and motivation. Moving in and out of different microcosms and surrounded by alternatives or challenged by new experiences, what do we learn? How do we respond to our own embodiment as we change and age, and as we experience others, embodied in multifarious ways? Are we jealous or joyless, stoical or long-suffering? Do we await a return to "normalcy" yet overlook present opportunities? Do we panic as we struggle to recreate a controlled and familiar environment? Do we prefer denial either by work or nostalgia? Or do we glory in being fully alive? The questions are important; we are called both to realize personal potentials and to relate creatively to the world and to people.

To spend our lives waiting for circumstances to change or unaware of the grace of the moment would be profligate and tragic; and to fail to notice God in other people and their cultures—their embodiments and their environments—would be careless and arrogant. The issues raised here concern our responsiveness to our own selves and to our environment, our readiness to be *surprised* by God, our adaptability to *unlikely* moments of grace, our ease or dis-ease with our *changing* bodies, and our ability to rejoice and give thanks for the revelation of God in the strange, the foreign, and the feared.

There is a danger, perhaps inherent in all socialization processes and certainly threatening many Christians, of reaching adulthood with a single, inflexible, orthodox attitude to God, truth, cosmos, and others (we might say a "spirituality"), which is assumed adequate for a lifetime. But all is change, and an unadapted spirituality will bring sclerosis rather than resilience. If one's spirituality is unreflectively understood to be in no need of major change but only of periodic adjustments and fine-tuning, how is acculturation, much less inculturation, to be effected? And without an adaptive spirituality, how is conversion—a changing of one's mind as much as of anything else—possible? And lest we imagine that there is no danger of monolithic spiritualities and stereotypical ways of being Christian, we have only to consider the specter of universal monoculturalism that lurks in Roman documents, liturgical prescriptions, the New Code of Canon Law, and the New Universal Catechism. Great care is needed in order to resist the static and universal which is at the expense of the dynamic and local.

To be inflexible in terms of adaption to other cultures or climates or to one's changing physical condition might be as deleterious to a life-giving spirituality as to be too accommodating to persons and places and regarding of one's changing personal needs. To spend one's life never still but constantly moving in and out of other cultural groups and their environmental contexts while all the time in the process from maturity to middle age to retirement to old age, and oscillating between health and sickness, strength and weakness, is to risk being alienated from a life-giving and peaceable way of being in the world and launched like a cork on a restless sea. And to carry around on our journey the baggage of all our presuppositions and points of reference, cherished way of being in the world, values, traditions, and beliefs, is to be encumbered to the point of incapacitation and blinkered to the point of blindness. Something has to change.

The conviction of an explicit mandate to replenish the earth and subdue it (Gen. 1:28) has led the post-Christian West—notwithstanding attempts to interpret this in terms of respect and social awareness—to the brink of environmental destruction, cultural impoverishment, and spiritual bankruptcy. Yet many of the self-styled religious maintain the conviction that consumerism and capitalism are not simply enlightened but actually responsible, if not literally God-given. The very recent and belated acknowledgment of the madness of such excesses has been due as much to the Western discovery of its own "nest fouling" and a consequent reordering of personal and national priorities as it is to the acquisition of wisdom from other traditions and cultures, or a rediscovery of social responsibilities. The West has notoriously—but not only in the past three centuries of Enlightenment, Positivism, and Manifest Destiny—rarely glimpsed, much less revered, the traditions of such peoples who had developed a highly integrated and respectful attitude toward the natural world, the supreme being, and the human community.[9]

But there are myriad examples of peoples who had discovered an "ecological spirituality" long before Francis of Assisi. They expressed personal embodiment as a participation in the public world of nature, culture, and the supernatural much in advance of voguish hippie culture or trendy liberalism. Indeed, as the West has become urbanized and cosmopolitan, whole generations have grown up with little or no direct contact with the earth or with the producers of natural resources; rather, the contemporary urbanite is a voracious consumer of "commodities," ignorant of their origin or the processes by which they came to be. Technocracies have dulled people's awareness of the world in which they live and of the symbiotic relationship that characterizes nature and society, irrespective of the latter's ignorance.

Among those cultures or societies so easily and pejoratively labeled "simple" or "primitive," symbiosis is part of experience. Any study of different social and ecological environments would disclose a high correlation between them and would identify distinguishable spiritualities. For where people have lived in groups over generations, they have come to terms not only with the demands of persons but of the environment itself. And any human group that has successfully survived on the earth can only have done so by means of some covenantal relationship with it.

People who live upon the earth and relate directly to it for nourishment and shelter know and respect its moods and rhythms. But those who become urbanized, individualistic, isolated, and consumeristic—or exploitative of the resources and environment that sustain their own and others' lives—know less of the earth and its moods and rhythms. This ignorance, compounded by arrogance, selfishness, and improvidence, is manifest in disregard or positive disrespect of the earth. People who live in urban ghettos or shanty towns, high-rise apartments or condominiums are strangers to skies or soils, ecosystems or seasons. Thus do "Western" or "technological" people become distanced from the ecology, from their relatedness to nature, and from their own humanity. Disassociated from and unaware of the earth as a living organism and used only to dealing with it as a repository for human needs, they easily come to treat themselves in a similar fashion, as machines needing occasional technical modifications rather than as embodied spirit, self-conscious and therefore responsible personally, socially, and cosmically.

Someone estranged from self and separated from the earth can also rather easily suffer another form of alienation, since the very people who live unattached to the earth and to nature tend to be either unattached to any location or set of relationships that could be called "home," or unrelated to notions of a personal God or supreme being or both. And since each of these notions is crucial for an understanding of integrated or embodied spirituality, they are worth pondering.

ECOLOGY AND THE MACROCOSM

Those living in an enclosed or tightly bounded world—a strong microcosm—would include prisoners or chronically hospitalized people, contemplative cenobites or army recruits, some tribal bands or isolated islanders. Compare the world of the jet-setter, the upwardly mobile graduate, or the nomad, whose world is unbounded and who lives within a macrocosm, able to reach out, cross boundaries, and move from place to place. In each case, a person will develop a distinctive relationship to the local and more distant worlds, and with that relationship will be some attitudes: to self and others, to the earth, and to the supreme being.

Consider the world of the forest-dwelling pygmy, with its face-to-face relationships and its boundedness, its strong microcosm and isolation from other worlds beyond. What do people know in detail about a universal God, or indeed of a universe? The world is populated by a proliferation of local intermediary spirits, and the supreme being is a shadowy figure who rarely impinges on daily reality yet underpins the universe as a whole. Consider, too, the world of a contemplative community, localized and fixed, strongly bounded and attached to particular traditions and liturgies. Insofar as it participates in a macrocosm rather than a microcosm, it will tend to relate to it as rather unreal or remote, unless specifically challenged by external agencies or by living memories of a world beyond.

But contrast this with the world of the traveler or the contemporary intellectual, the one transported in an airplane, the other in an armchair. Such a person lives in a very weak microcosm, or breaks free of it rather easily, to roam in the world beyond, whether of people and places or of ideas. This is the person who might with relative ease detach from early socialization, understanding, and belief, as alternative realities and ranges of human response become familiar. Within the microcosm, there is effectively only one reality and a minimum of ways of being in the world; beyond, in the macrocosm, reality seems multiple, truth relativized, and there are many ways of being in the world.

Although a person within a strong microcosm has little choice and lives in high conformity, discovering meaning locally and not meeting the supreme being as a quotidian experience, such a one is also rooted, finding identity through local relationships. For someone in a weakly bounded microcosm, the whole world is indeed a stage; yet the tendency might be to treat others not as fellow actors but as anonymous and therefore unrelated. In the macrocosm one may pass, if not unnoticed then probably not called to account, if not free to believe or behave independently then probably not called to community. Whoever roams in the macrocosm is free to experience many worlds but may feel alienated from any particular world. Yet those whose loyalties are not tied to a local group may seem adrift on an open sea. Life in the macrocosm may open one to a more direct understanding of the ways of nature or God, or just as easily produce a life of profligacy or irresponsibility, alienation from self, from earth, or from the supreme being. "Friends of the Earth" may try to bond with the universe and all humanity as they strive for a life integrated between microcosm and macrocosm, but the modern traveler, free to browse globally, may easily fail to integrate and to respect, and come only to despoil nature and to blaspheme God.

ECOLOGY AND THE MICROCOSM

There is a further issue, that of the appropriation of a sense of "home" as people contextualize themselves relative to microcosm and macrocosm, earth and God, and as variables of mobility and responsibility, embodiment and worship are considered.

Highly mobile people in today's world may be prone not only to learning wonderful things about other cultures, to conversion in spirituality, and to increase in wisdom, but also to a certain atrophy, an unhealthy detachment from the earth and from people, and a failure to benefit from changes occurring in their own persons and external environment. The result would be a disintegration of one's spirituality or way of being in the world that, given the inestimable advantage of breaking through one's microcosm and living among others within the macrocosm, would be tragic and unnecessary. Many people — particularly ministers and especially missionaries — may not be availing themselves of splendid opportunities for deepening their spirituality as they deepen their experiences, and of coming closer to peace and to God as they come closer to old age and death.

Assuming we are able to be flexible and creative in the face of change, whether physical, geographical, or emotional, our travels across the earth and our embodiment that responds to time and circumstance will contribute to a maturing spirituality. This is easy to say. But adaptability does not appear to characterize the majority of human beings; rather predictability, inflexibility, and inertia seem to constrain us, and there develops a real tension between our responsiveness to the wider world and our limitations as culture-bound people.

Many highly urbanized and mobile individuals may lose touch with themselves and their roots due to the demands of a pluralistic and cosmopolitan life-style. Those who are "all things to all people" and "here today, gone tomorrow" may make a virtue of being free and unattached, but to the detriment of their own identity. How can a person develop a relationship with the world, if not through living persons and the living earth? And how are relationships possible if nothing is stable? It is difficult to see how one can be a child of the universe without also being related to some particular locale: Even nomads stay within a specific environment or ecosystem, rather than traveling aimlessly or as refugees. To be detached from the world—truly physically detached and not consciously dependent on it—means to be without certain relationships and thus without a sense of responsibility toward or for it. To be detached in this way is to be alienated from one's own embodiment and so forget one's earthiness and rootedness and interdependence. Conversely, a spirituality that promotes physical control over relaxation or abandonment tends to relate to the macrocosm with the same kind of dominance it exercises in relation to the microcosm.

TRADITIONS OF WISDOM

Unless we can come to terms simply and respectfully with other cultures and values, spiritualities and environments, physical and emotional states, we are as far from fulfilling our potential and being converted as if we were to stay at home, catatonic. But we can only do that if we accept that wisdom and grace and truth are indeed in other people, their worlds, and their ways of being in the world.

If we think that people beyond the Judeo-Christian tradition—or perhaps beyond the so-called Great World Religions—have genuine religious insights, spirituality, and knowledge of God, then we might be more open to their own particular *way of knowing and experiencing* those insights and that spirituality and knowledge. Or if we respect their own integrated attitude to the world in which they live—to the earth and themselves and each other—we might infer more about their own religious insights, spirituality, and knowledge. But our own social construction of reality and anthropomorphization of God tend effectively to screen other realities and other perceptions of God from our vision. And since attitudes to embodiment (that is, tolerance or repression, enjoyment or discipline of physicality and physical processes) and to the environment tend to be built upon attitudes to social worlds, we may have to reconstruct the latter if our own spirituality (our way of being in the world with God) is to be redeemed and live.

In a world of telecommunications and high mobility, we have less and less excuse both for failing to learn from others and for failing to adapt our spirituality to our environment and embodiment. To be old and sick in Katmandu is presumably different from being young and healthy in Acapulco. To be a female academic in Harvard is presumably different from being a homeless male on the streets of Chicago. And to be a stranger in a strange land is presumably different from sitting around one's own fireside with friends. A culture that spawns thousands of young addicts who abuse bodies and minds but think themselves invincible is not surprisingly the very culture that abuses the environment but believes itself capable of fixing anything that temporarily malfunctions. The way people treat each other and their world tends to be mirrored in the way they treat themselves. And if we can find societies that respect their environment and each other, then we will be able to identify societies whose members still respect themselves and their bodies. Then perhaps not only will we learn from others' wisdom but also remind ourselves of the riches in our own traditions that are in grave danger of being forgotten under the welter of novelties produced by our insatiable society.[10]

Finally, a suggestion and a question. The suggestion is that unless we know how to care for our world, we will forget how to care for ourselves in a creative and nurturing fashion. Those who care for their environment seem able to acknowledge their own mortality, while those who abuse it seem also committed to a denial of death. Perhaps as people rediscover how to face their own mortality, thus converting them from nihilism or secularism and reminding them of traditions that relate people to the Creator, they will be able to live with their limitations. Then it might be more possible to invest in a future that will not include them but will include their descendants and the earth. Denial of death is destructive of self and of environment, while acceptance of mortality may produce attitudes of nurturing both for self and for the world, or what I have called an "ecological spirituality."

And the question: If we were asked, as Martin Luther was, what we would do if we knew the earth would end tomorrow, how might we respond?

NOTES

1. "Spirituality" is used here in a generic or descriptive rather than a technical sense, to contrast with simple physicality. But it implies a holistic approach to life, in which a person's stance relative to the supreme being is not easily isolated from day-to-day pursuits, and in which an embodied person is not simply a physical entity but a spiritual being.

2. This paper is about suggestions, not about rules. It does not take a deterministic view of life but rather suggests trends or hypotheses for further consideration and testing.

3. *See* Mary Douglas, *Natural Symbols* (Harmondsworth: Penguin Books, 1970). Peter Brown, *The Body and Society* (New York: Columbia University Press, 1988), discusses the theme of sexual renunciation and the early centuries of the Church.

4. A particularly illuminating study is Clifford Geertz's *Agricultural Involution* (Berkeley: University of California, 1963). He shows how economic and political factors themselves shaped Javanese cultural forms, producing a manifestation of embodiment marked by ghostliness and theatricality.

5. Robin Horton has developed the thesis of the microcosm and the macrocosm, its relative strength and weakness, and the relationship between these variables and attitudes to local spirits or the supreme being. *See* his "African Conversion," *Africa* (1971): 85–108; "On the Rationality of Conversion," *Africa* (1975): 219–35.

6. Douglas, pp. 93–112.

7. A splendid and engrossing account is Richard Katz's *Boiling Energy* (Cambridge, Mass.: Harvard University Press, 1982) which describes spirit possession among the Kalahari Bushmen, the !Kung.

8. Consider the tension between the Magisterium of the Roman Catholic

Church today and reaction of many of the faithful; or more generally, the preoccupation with sex and sexuality in Western culture.

9. *See* Keith Thomas, *Man and the Natural Environment* (New York: Pantheon,
1983) which is a fine social history of contemporary attitudes to the environment
and the human community.

10. *See* Douglas: "the more social change, the more radical revision of cosmol-
ogies, the more conversion phenomena" (p. 180).

5

Interiority and the "Universe of Discourse"

CARL F. STARKLOFF, SJ

Recently a fellow Jesuit recounted to me a fascinating anecdote that bears directly on the point of the present essay. The incident he described took place during a visit to Australia for the purpose of conducting workshops in spirituality. While there, he was asked by a colleague who works among aboriginal people to facilitate a "sin-history, grace-history" session involving aboriginal persons and white church ministers. The long-range objective of the conversation was to establish a process of reconciliation. As the visitor tells it, he was startled at what occurred in the course of the session. The Euro-Australian people found it relatively easy to enter into the project, and to share their respective stories. The aboriginals, however (at least by this person's judgment), were scarcely able at all to discourse on a history of personal sin, and those who did so talked mostly about what had happened to them or to their ancestors at the hands of the Europeans.

As I reflected on the situation as it was described, my own reaction was that the outcome should not have been surprising, for a combination of reasons. To begin with, the native people of that land, perhaps even more emphatically than those of North America, had probably been living witnesses to or recipients of avalanches of European prejudice, racism, and oppression. There are accounts of group massacres of aborigines even in mid-twentieth century. The reality was probably also engraved in their memories from the oral traditions passed on by their elders. Related to this fact would no doubt have been the deeply damaged self-esteem wrought by a lifetime of humiliations. An authentic, healthy "sense of sin" would require, among other qualities, a strong sense of self.

Finally, and perhaps most profoundly from the cultural point of view, would be the likelihood that the church persons in this conversation were relating to persons coming from a background in a "shame culture" rather than in a "sin culture," such as Europeans are accustomed to. All of these factors I surmised from my own fairly brief acquaintance—totaling about two months—with Australian aboriginal people, from other similar experiences, and from study, would loom large in any reconciliation dialogue.

This labor of getting to know and understand the inner thoughts and feelings of persons in other cultures is a relatively new phenomenon, arising along with the nineteenth-century concept of culture. Even as recently as the 1950s, when I was first assigned to work among the native people in the United States, no effort was put into training me to understand them in their own uniqueness. When I hear aspiring missionaries even today admit to having no skills for such understanding, I become annoyed. And yet, that was my own story exactly! Worse, the churches have lagged behind the "secular sciences" in this matter. It is my hope that the present essay might indicate ways in which my experiences, as well as the reading of literary, missiological, and anthropological thinkers, have helped me deal with the lacuna to which I refer.

THE IMPORTANCE OF CULTURAL ANALYSIS

Missiologist David Hesselgrave has argued for the importance of discerning whether a people among whom one works belongs to a shame culture or to a guilt culture. Citing Ruth Benedict, Hesselgrave describes a guilt culture as one in which "the child takes the values of the parent as its own and learns to act as if the parent were present even when the parent is absent" (Hesselgrave 1983:463). In this system, God is understood as backing up the "parent" and is primarily concerned with moral behavior. Benedict describes a shame culture, on the other hand, as one "in which ideal behavior is determined by an elaborate system of obligations to the larger society and its included groups" (464). While I have problems with Hesselgrave's evangelical propensity to seek out chinks in a culture's armor into which to insert the sword of the Word of God, his essay came readily to mind when I heard the above story. He has made an important point.

Canadian historian Cornelius Jaenen recounts historical accounts describing a similar shame culture, in writing about the encounter between North American natives and Europeans in the sixteenth and seventeenth centuries. He writes, "Furthermore, the lack of any general concepts of personal sin or blame, such as pervaded the self-regarding ideologies of the Europeans, led the Amerindians to regard success or failure of the individual as the result of external forces playing upon him" (Jaenen 1976:115). Accordingly, native leaders were much more inclined to blame their problems on the coming of the Europeans, even when perhaps the connection would not be so evident to the outsiders. Jaenen's whole volume is an interesting account of similar sources of misunderstanding between the conflicting cultures.

It is this problem of intercultural understanding of motives that concerns me in the present article, especially because the missionaries involved in these encounters come to aboriginal societies as representatives of a "universalist" religion as well as an imperialist society. It is thus the people of my own historical background who initiated the possibilities both of exchange and communication, as well as of conflict. If our spirituality is indeed universal in its aspirations, then there lies upon us a serious duty to investigate the sources of contemporary problems in communication.

Ignatius Loyola has bequeathed to us a priceless piece of counsel regarding the relationship between a director of his Spiritual Exercises and the one currently passing through them as an "exercitant." In a short section now called "Presupposition," Loyola prescribes a three-moment communication process. He first "presupposes" that every good Christian is more prepared to interpret another's viewpoint favorably than to condemn it. Secondly, he writes that if one is unable to accept another's viewpoint, one must carefully inquire of the other how the person understands that viewpoint. Finally, only having made such painstaking efforts to interpret, and still being unable to agree, might one then strive to correct the other (Puhl 1951:11). What Ignatius intended in the context of the Exercises, and thus not really providing for the possibility of significant culture differences between the persons, I am here seeking to implement in a cross-cultural context. The fundamental question inspiring this essay is: How can I come to understand better the "interiority" or inner life and motivation of persons with whom I seek spiritual dialogue and cooperation? Such a conversation presupposes, of course, that I am not invading the other's inner life and desecrating the fundamental mystery of the human person, but that I have been accepted as a conversation partner.

As a basic statement on conversation between "modern" persons and "primal" persons, I have found none more profound than what comes to us from literary critic Northrop Frye. At one point Frye argues on behalf of metaphorical and mythical thinking (which is more common to primal or tribal societies), and against "the naive belief in progress which identifies the primitive with the outmoded" (Frye 1982:23). It is a graver error, moreover, to consider myth a mistaken attempt at conceptual thinking; metaphor and myth are enduring modes of expression (23). Elsewhere Frye writes that in the dialogue between the modern Western and the primitive, we must transcend mere "bilingual dictionary" methods of conversation. We must rather seek to discover the ground of symbolic structure. Thus, it is possible, with patience and sympathy, to work "to disentangle one's own mental processes from the swaddling clothes of their native syntax" (Frye 1978:72). But this whole process calls for a demanding exchange in the search for a comprehensible and communicable inner structure.

Northrop Frye is breaking a lance here against most of nineteenth-century evolutionary thought, rejecting the extravagant dichotomies set up between primitives and moderns by Levy-Bruhl, as well as the intellectualistic evolutionarism of Edward B. Tylor. In this he has much contemporary anthropology on his side in such thinkers as Claude Levi-Strauss, Adolf Jensen, and Robert Lowie. Levi-Strauss, despite all the faults charged to him, was convinced of the sophistication of the "savage mind" and spent his entire life attempting to support this argument. (See especially Levi-Strauss 1966, Ch. 1.) Levi-Strauss's optimistic obsession might hopefully become at least a hopeful preoccupation of all Christian missionaries!

Adolf Jensen, in turn, defended "the basic changelessness of the nature of [man] from the moment that the word [man] can be justifiably applied to him" (Jensen 1963:39). Jensen, taking his cue from the cultural historical school, believed that there is no fundamental difference between primitive people and moderns in regard to spiritual matters. Any conversation here must be treated from the perspective of a knowledge of the culture to which one is relating (25). It was unthinkable for Jensen that the creators of these primitive forms of expression should be any less human than himself, especially seeing that these persons possessed "a remarkable and wise regimen of life and were technologically and mechanically gifted" (262).

Lowie, like Jensen, steadfastly refused to separate religious experience from its cultural context. Likewise, he maintained the basic equality of all members of the human species. He was even loathe to categorically deny the much-criticized hypothesis of the Catholic anthropologist Wilhelm Schmidt that the "rudest societies" practiced a high form of prayer and believed in an ethical deity (Lowie 1970:323).

My point in referring to the above scholars is to support the belief that cross-cultural understanding of another's interior life is possible, but not without long personal acquaintance, study, and infinitely patient dialogue.[1] The tension in the search for understanding in one sense reflects the tension between universality and particularity within Christianity and in all interreligious dialogue. Universality is presupposed in the Christian belief in a common humanity; it is likewise susceptible to a certain naive romanticism or to a facile (and one-sided) inference that one culture's experience is just like that of another. It can even fall into the primitive trap of believing that contemporary aboriginal cultures are no different from archaic cultures. Here we must lift up the emphasis on particularity (appreciation for different concrete cultures) if we are to work toward empathy and understanding of different values and historical perspectives.

INTERIORITY

I do not wish to complicate the idea of interiority, however difficult it may be to grasp how it functions in diverse cultures and eras. In its simplest meaning, let us take it as the inner experience of mind, heart, and spirit, not necessarily as separate "faculties," but as differing focuses of the person. The Danish philosopher Kierkegaard was perhaps the most passionate defender of individual interiority and a passionate "inwardness" that throws each individual upon his or her own unique relationship with God.

To truly love another is to respect his or her inwardness, and to despise another's unique inwardness is the sin of "pettiness" (Kierkegaard 1946: 221).

Ignatius Loyola had written this counsel into his Exercises long before, especially in the fifteenth to seventeenth annotations, which instruct the retreat director to respect the interaction between the Creator and the creature. The spiritual director must not intrude with attempts to sway choices, or inquire into another's interior sins, but must rather act as a certain "balance at equilibrium" as the other strives to come to a decision (Puhl 1951:6–7).

In our own era, we now recognize a kind of individualism in the spiritual counsels of Kierkegaard, and even of Ignatius, although the context he created for spiritual direction was actually quite social. But more to our point here is that both Ignatius and Kierkegaard presupposed a common cultural communication in their ideas of spiritual discourse, whether in the medium of spiritual direction, preaching, or writing. Thus, it becomes necessary here to contextualize the basic values of Kierkegaard and Loyola — interiority (Kierkegaard) and concern to establish communication in the other (Ignatius) — into a cross-cultural methodology. Our emphasis on the contemporary appreciation of cultural uniqueness calls for a reflection process prior to direct spiritual communication (which, of course, Kierkegaard constantly supported within his own context).

To establish a cross-cultural dialogue in spiritual interchange would mean, for example, that any narrating of one's "history of sin" would have to depend on how one sees moral conduct and its relationship to a transcendent deity. Thus, in discussion with Arapaho elders, I came to learn that their tradition focused on moral offense as "horizontal," or as actions against one's fellow human beings or fellow tribespersons, rather than against the "One-over-all-things" (who we now call "God"). These elders, of course, had themselves been trained in the Christian idea of personal sin, but they were still aware that their culture had a different conception. I found myself reflecting on how, had I been a missionary among them a century earlier, I might have conversed with them about values. Would I have felt constrained to stress the guilt-culture notion over that of the shame culture? Even as we conversed, I realized that their deep and internalized sense of tribal solidarity was a counterweight to my own more privatized sense of sin and guilt. I was learning something of the psychological and intellectual asceticism necessary for truly meaningful cross-cultural value exchange.

INTERIORITY, SPIRITUALITY, AND SYMBOLISM

I will not enter into further elaboration of the already superabundant supply of theories of symbolism. But it is important here at least to discuss the way in which a knowledge of symbolism can deeply affect one's expe-

rience in cross-cultural exchange. Anthropologists and religion scholars
have dwelt endlessly on the relationship between dynamism and animism,
magic and religion, fetishism and symbolism. But to illustrate the critical
role symbolism has in common religious experience, I would simply call
attention to the great Christian spiritual writer Evelyn Underhill, to both
her profundity and to her limitation in the matter of symbol. She writes,

> Religion . . . can never entirely divorce herself from magic; for her rituals and
> sacraments must have, if they are to be successful in their appeal to the mind,
> a certain magical character. All persons who are naturally drawn towards the
> ceremonial aspect of religion are acknowledging the strange power of subtle
> rhythms, symbolic words and movements, over the human will (Underhill
> 1961:163).

Further on she writes, "the business of the Church is to appeal to the
whole [man], as she finds him living in a world of sense. She would be
hardly adequate to this task did she neglect the powerful weapons which
the occultist has developed for his own ends" (164).

Finally, Underhill returns to the same kind of respect for the creator–
creature relationship that we see in Kierkegaard and Ignatius Loyola. The
Church, she argues, cannot "extract finality from a method which does not
really seek after ultimate things" (164). That is, the Church may teach
values and seek to move feelings, but she cannot do the job of God within
the individual. Quoting Coventry Patmore, she writes, "The work of the
Church ends where the knowledge of God begins" (164). Again, like Loyola
and Kierkegaard, Underhill gives a vivid defense of symbolism and discourse, while reminding us of its limitations. And, also like these two, she
has not explored the problem of culture in religious discourse.

I am arguing that it is possible for the Church to work at filling the
lacuna between respect for personal and cultural uniqueness and the bearing of witness, and that this may be done by appreciating that there is
witness to be borne on both sides. What Underhill has begun as a defense
of symbolism in religious communication, we must advance through the
further effort to understand the function of symbol in the interiority of the
other culture.

One anthropologist who can guide us more deeply into this forest of
symbolism (even though the image is Victor Turner's) is Clifford Geertz.
Geertz sees that the heart of religion is neither metaphysics nor ethics; its
moral vitality is rather "in the fidelity with which it expresses the fundamental nature of reality" (Geertz 1973:126). That is, religion is, among
many other things, the attempt to "conserve the fund of general meanings
in terms of which each individual interprets [his or her] experience and
organizes [his or her] conduct" (127). For Geertz, the only way that meaning can be "stored" is in symbols, because they serve to synthesize a people's
worldview and ethos. In addition he stresses that, "The force of a religion

in supporting social values rests, then, on the ability of its symbols to formulate a world in which those values, as well as the forces opposing their realization, are fundamental ingredients" (127). The dialogue demanded in order to appreciate this function of symbolism, then, must become a part of the spirituality furthered by the Christian writers I have discussed.

Rather than employ Geertz's examples to illustrate his point, I will describe my own experience of native North American Christians who have integrated their meanings, both tribal and Christian, by means of traditional but adapted symbols. It is especially significant that, having been a theology teacher and even an occasional spiritual guide to several of these persons, I have found myself often receiving direction from them as they describe these manifestations of their symbolic life and values.

Peter Manitowabe is an Ojibway from Manitoulin Island in Lake Huron, who was ordained deacon some five years ago after his years of formation in the ministries program at Anishinabe Spiritual Centre. Since entering into ministry more fully, Peter has integrated his own program of spiritual direction and healing for his people around the symbol of the medicine wheel—common in varying forms to all Native Peoples of North America. He locates all the values he seeks to inculcate—drawing both from native and imported teachings—around and within the wheel. He has also been fascinated by the now popular "pastoral circle" used so often in social analysis, and has adapted it to his own circle.

Another Ojibway minister is Margaret Toulouse, also from the general Manitoulin area, who has developed similar creative usages of traditional symbolism. She has likewise worked out a detailed ordering of ideal values on the medicine wheel, especially in her work as a family counselor. She has also delivered lectures to audiences of theological students and laypersons outside the native community. Moreover, she has also revived the sweat lodge with the help of traditional native spiritual leaders, and now conducts the ceremony herself in a Christian context. Again, this woman, with whom I began as a teacher, has often been my teacher and guide in the discovery of the values of aboriginal symbol and the meaning it holds for my own life. I have learned that spirituality is more a gift than a product of muscle, even though many native ascetical practices could also be interpreted as spiritual athleticism!

A third Ojibway spiritual leader is Walter Linklater of Thunder Bay, Ontario, a counselor and educator. The circle also has its unique place in Walter's life, being employed as a unifying symbol in group reconciliation processes. In this case, the wheel is literally a human circle, into which Linklater assembles participants, either outdoors around a fire or indoors around a large candle. Appropriate times may be either at dawn or very late at night. Participants are urged to do most of the talking and sharing, but the leader himself will speak about how he has integrated into his circle the threefold value system of the seven teachings of the elders, the twelve steps of Alcoholics Anonymous, and the Ten Commandments. Whether the circle here is an instance of dynamism, animism, or symbolism becomes an academic question. What has happened is that spiritual communication has become an authentic event.

The above are only three outstanding examples among many. Other native Christian leaders integrate values around pipe ceremonies, incensing rituals, sweat lodges, nature walks to obtain healing herbs, and in one case in the form of a medicine lodge. These persons' relationships with the Creator and with their environment have been shared with their own people and have educated me in my own "intrareligious dialogue." Symbols have served to admit us who are otherwise outsiders into the value systems and interior experiences of native people.

MUTUAL SPIRITUAL DIRECTION

From the outset, I have considered this essay not as an exploration of how we as Euro-North American Christians might "give spiritual direction" across cultures, but rather how bridges might be built between cultures to allow passing over from and to both sides. In fact, while I have spent many years of ministry giving "pastoral counseling" to many native persons, when "spiritual direction" is in question, I have been more on the receiving than the giving end. Seeking to give a name to the kind of spirituality and theology I have been learning in such exchanges, I am impressed by the happy phrase of Chinese theologian C. S. Song—"third-eye theology." This is an expression intended to mediate the tension between east-west experience, between the intellectual and intuitive, between the wrongly dichotomized "creation" and "redemption" theologies. Song's method applies as well to the dialogue between the modern and the primal worldviews. We can apply his argument to our discussion: "Christian theology in Asia cannot fulfill its task until it constructs a universe of discourse with other faiths in the quest for a deeper understanding and experience of God, human beings and the world" (Song 1979:76).

The third eye is a concept taken especially from Buddhist tradition. It is "a power of perception and insight that enables [theologians] to grasp the meaning under the surface of things and phenomena" (xi). With this we learn to share the common visions and aspirations of the neighbor (21). The third eye serves to overcome the "darkness of Being" and the darkness separating Christian from other Asian spiritualities (22).

I would suggest that third-eye theology (and spirituality) is a way in which to reverence the profound mystery—the fullness of being that defies all attempts at systems and formulation—in the other. While I do not sympathize with facile lapses into "apophatic" mysticism in the face of theological problems (which are not the same as mystery!), I support the argument that intercultural dialogue demands a certain suspension of the critical faculty as a kind of phenomenological *epoche.*

As I have observed this approach, I have at times found, paradoxically, that native partners in a discussion will bring up important speculative questions. I recall the remark of an Arapaho elder some years ago during a discussion about what title to assign to Jesus in the native language. "Let's remember first," he asserted, "that the Big Boss is God!" I have seldom been involved in a better christological or trinitarian discussion than the one that ensued. But the point is that the third eye is in operation here as we seek to mediate the tensions.

One of my longest-standing recollections involves an earlier interest in learning how to deal with spiritual visions and auditions among aboriginal peoples. One would often hear them speak about seeing or hearing communications from the other realm. Common sense, of course, dictated to me that I should not conceive these experiences in a literal, physical sense. But another side of me prompted, "Don't be so sure of that! We could be dealing with an entirely different meaning of spiritual faculties here." But it was a statement from an elder that activated my third eye to enable it to gaze upon the truth at issue. Pointing to his heart, he advised, "What counts is what happens here." The theologian in me eventually recalled what Karl Rahner was attempting to understand in applying his own transcendental method to the matter of visions (Rahner 1964:87–188).

Again, I recall the point made by another spiritual leader advising on how one is to relate to different spirits that might present themselves when one is fasting in the wilderness, especially if they seemed to be hostile spirits. "What you have to do is tell them why you went out there in the first place—to fulfill a vow." As I heard this, I remembered the response attributed to St. Bernard when he was tempted to give up his calling: "I did not come here for you; neither will I leave for you!" Any argument over whether the spirits are "real" or "projected" vanishes in the face of what is essential when on an important quest: It is the quest itself that is important. I was able to make use of such advice pastorally on several occasions when native persons sought help on how to deal with spirit visitations, especially of dead relatives: "If they are unfriendly spirits, tell them that Jesus is stronger than they are. If they are relatives, maybe they just want your prayers."

In aboriginal experience, the categories of animate and inanimate (in many languages a third "gender" distinction), involve a third-eye mysticism that sees into the communicative power not only in animal and vegetable life, but in minerals as well. Ojibway greet each heated rock brought into the sweat lodge with "Boojou, Mishomis!" or "Hello, Grandfather!" But the most delightful of anecdotes around this experience comes to us from the anthropologist Irving Hallowell. When he asked an Ojibway elder, "Are all the stones we see about us here alive?" the old man answered, "No! But some are" (Hallowell 1975:147–49). To the perceptive Hallowell, this response communicated that the elder was articulating not a "consciously formulated theory" about stones, but simply stating that, in some situations, stones were seen to be animate. What was significant to the speaker was the spiritual value of the experience.

Perhaps even more significant experiences of third-eye attitudes belong to the modern history of aboriginal peoples in the struggle to relate to the contemporary environment. One of the great tragedies of history is highlighted when we hear or read about how aboriginal spiritual leaders abandoned their "medicines" after being overwhelmed by superior colonial force. Now, however, in these times of native protest against exploitation, more "sophisticated" aboriginal leaders locate the problem where it belongs—in imperialist aggression. Nonetheless, these leaders have never failed, in my experience, to set their legal and political protests within a native ritual. The observer participating in such events does well simply to enter into the experience, even if intending to continue the tiresome academic debate about applying Marxist categories to popular religiosity among the oppressed.

One such example has been dramatically evident among the Teme Augama Anishnabai Ojibways of northern Ontario during their long and painful protest vigil and struggle to block construction of the Red Squirrel Road at the entrance to the Temagami Wilderness Area. All sympathetic visitors are welcomed, and all protests are begun, with a rite of prayer with sweet grass, cedar, or tobacco incense. The power to persevere through bitterly cold winters in the forest has been enhanced not only by a passion for justice and the environment, but by a sense of the Creator in their midst.

A similar mediation between political savvy and primal spiritual power was evident to me during visits among the Australian aborigines of the Kimberley Region. These ancient peoples have grown extremely conscientized about their rightful place on the land and about the rape of the land by diamond mines and other prospectors. But they too have continued to dwell within the spiritual environment of the problem, even in the midst of legal battles and public protests.

For example, a classic aboriginal belief adheres to an ancient and measureless "dream time" when the creative beings were powerful and gave the people their land and traditions. I was impressed with this fact when an aboriginal elder offered to give me a ride in his pickup out to the place of his "dreaming." The site was a beautiful and pastoral setting where a small river flowed into a clear pool set in the cradle of a small bluff. Trees and other plants shielded the area from the sun and kept it fresh. There were some petroglyphs on the wall of the bluff. As we left the enchanted area, my host spoke to me in a very contemporary idiom: "This is our culture. We won't let them take it away from us!" But the power of the dream time is essential in their campaign. It takes a third eye to understand how deeply interior this belief is.

CONCLUSION

I need not dwell here on the current trends in feminist and environmental theology to emphasize relational values and the values of companionship between humans and nature. I have found myself strongly affected by the more reflective of these theologies, as well as by the sense of the tension between the more cerebral and the more intuitive aspects of theological and spiritual communication. We are not doing our job as theologians or spiritual leaders or ministers if we dismiss either pole of this tension. One gift to such persons from aboriginal dialogue partners is to call them to "dwell" within the tension, by being both more contemplative and more reflective—each in its own time.

Over the last fifteen years, I have been privileged to sit at the feet of the wise among aboriginal leaders, probably more often than they have sat at my feet. In this way I have acquired both valuable information and healing unction. Still, I am aware that the present situation is a highly syncretistic one: That is, many elements, both ancient and modern, have been "poured together" in such a way as to lead to the present dialogue. Thus, we see the give-and-take possibility in spiritual direction. For my part, I have been able to share with native ministers and candidates—not always with lucidity or power, I realize—a great deal of theological reflection on the dialogue. I have also witnessed how these persons have so often brought into play their own third eye in the effort to place my teaching and that of others within their own world situation.

Such usages have returned in many forms. There is, for example, the Lord's Prayer within native ceremonies and the powerful figure of the crucified Jesus in Blake Debossige's painting "The Tree of Life." There is Leland Bell's creation of the Stations of the Cross, accompanied by his own interpretation, in the Church of the Immaculate Conception in West Bay on Manitoulin Island (cf. Leach, Humbert, Bell 1989). They have come in the form of wise and experienced pastoral counseling given by Deacon Dominic Eshkakogan in carefully measured instructions to his people on how to relate to the "Shaking Tent" ceremony. They come in the form of charismatic prayer gatherings that render present the Father, Son, and the Holy Spirit, as well as Kateri Tekakwitha and Joseph Chiwatenhwa and other saints in occasions of healing and mutual exhortation.

Cross-cultural dialogue is then not merely an interchange of two separate worldviews. It is in itself a spiritual event of the coming together of many experiences in a new "universe of discourse" in which we benefit from a sharing in the other's interiority. As we engage in this, we realize that not all the rocks are alive. But some may be.

NOTES

1. On reflection, I believe that my method, at least at this stage, is not unlike that of Wilfred Cantwell Smith (Smith 1981, ch. 4 esp.).

REFERENCES

Frye, Northrop. (1978). "Myth as Information." In Robert D. Denham, ed. *Northrop Frye on Culture and Literature*. Chicago: University of Chicago Press.

———. (1982). *The Great Code: The Bible and Literature.* Toronto: Academic Press.

Geertz, Clifford. (1973). *The Interpretation of Cultures.* New York: Basic Books.

Hallowell, A. Irving. (1975). "Ojibway Ontology, Behavior and World Tedlock." *Voices from the American Earth.* New York: Liveright, pp. 141–78.

Hesselgrave, David. (1983). "Missionary Elenctics and Guilt and Shame." *Missiology* 11 (October, 1983): 463–83.

Jaenen, Cornelius J. (1976). *Friend and Foe: Aspects of French-Amerindian Culture Contact in the Sixteenth and Seventeenth Centuries.* New York: Columbia University Press.

Jensen, Adolf E. (1963). *Myth and Cult Among Primitive Peoples.* Trans. Marianna Tax Choldin and Wolfgang Weisleder. Chicago: University of Chicago Press.

Kierkegaard, Søren. (1946). *Works of Love.* Lillian and Marvin Swenson, eds. Princeton, N.J.: Princeton University Press.

Leach, George, S.J., Greg Humbert, and Leland Bell. (1989). *Beedahbun: First Light of Dawn.* North Bay, Ont.: Tomiko.

Levi-Strauss, Claude. (1966). *The Savage Mind.* Chicago: University of Chicago Press.

Lowie, Robert A. (1970). *Primitive Religion.* New York: Liveright, PB.

Puhl, Louis J., S.J. (1951). *The Spiritual Exercises of St. Ignatius Loyola.* Chicago: Loyola University Press.

Rahner, Karl, S.J. (1964). "Visions and Prophecies." Trans. Charles H. Henkey and Richard Strachan. *Inquiries.* New York: Herder and Herder.

Smith, Wilfred Cantwell. (1981). *Towards a World Theology: Faith and the Comparative History of Religion.* Philadelphia: Westminster Press.

Song, Choan-Seng. (1979). *Third-Eye Theology: Theology in Formation in Asian Settings.* Maryknoll, N.Y.: Orbis Books. Revised edition 1991.

Underhill, Evelyn. (1961). *Mysticism: A Study in the Nature and Development of Man's Spiritual Consciousness.* New York: E.P. Dutton.

6

Going Deep to the Truth:
Thomas Merton and Spiritual Direction
in a Cross-Cultural Context

CONRAD C. HOOVER, CO

Thomas Merton was a person of prayer who was remarkably in touch with events and conditions of the world from within the confines of his monastic enclosure. His reflections on contemplation and the spiritual life are read the world over. He was wonderfully open to persons and ideas alien to his accustomed limited range of experience. Nor was he threatened by what was new and different.

Although Thomas Merton wrote about spiritual direction, he never specifically addressed the issue of direction in a cross-cultural context. But he was fascinated by other cultures and learned from diverse experiences of God. His Christian faith was not threatened because he knew his center in the God whom he experienced in his Roman Catholic monastic community. Indeed he could write in his journal toward the end of his life, "My ideas are always changing, always moving around one center, and I am always seeing that center from somewhere else."[1] Thus, Merton began with the conviction that there is an essential unity bonding all humanity that precedes attempts to categorize and systematize. This unity both points to the possibility of approach and dialogue with one another and also suggests an agenda for spiritual practice.

In *Conjectures of a Guilty Bystander*, Merton wrote that "[W]e must contain all divided worlds in ourselves and transcend them in Christ."[2] Further, in the 1965 Japanese edition of *Seeds of Contemplation* he wrote in stunning words about "the way" of the wise where some persons from many diverse "ancient and traditional societies" plumb the depths of meaning and experience them for all the rest of us:

... they would so to speak bring together in themselves the divisions or complications that confused the life of their fellows. By healing the divisions in themselves they would help the divisions of the whole world. They would realize in themselves that unity which is at the same time the highest action and the purest rest, true knowledge and self-less love, beyond knowledge in emptiness and unknowing; a willing beyond will in apparent non-activity.[3]

Deep within there is the inner ground of the contemplative experience, where personal authenticity and unity are to be found, and this is a possibility for all people. By moving down into the depths of themselves in the solitude, they discover the true ground of being that is "universal love," and the paradox is that this ground of love "is the undivided unity of love for which there is no number."[4] It is in this solitude that a person is at one and the same time most alone before God and also most united with others in love. There is an essential unity both beyond and before our reasoning and our activity that opens the way.

Thomas Merton dealt with this paradox of the universal in the particular in many of his writings, and he discussed it in one of the most significant talks of his Asian journey. In an informal address to monks, he spoke of the communication that is possible at the deepest level of being, and said that in this experience "communion" is already present. He concluded by saying: "My dear brothers, we are already one. But we imagine that we are not. And what we have to recover is our original unity. What we have to be is what we already are."[5]

The ecumenical encounter for Merton began with this conviction that there was an essential unity of all human beings that could be realized in the contemplative experience and that was grounded deep within in the common ground of love. The place to begin was to honor the reality of the person as he or she was and in the integrity of his or her own journey. If one began there, then there was much to learn from one another.

At the same time for Merton, there was also the conviction that the contemplative experience was already embedded in the traditions of all peoples. Merton felt that wherever life itself exists, there the contemplative vocation is applicable and of great benefit.[6] If the deepest experiences of life have significance, where there are dreams for the future, where there is love and pain mingled with happiness, then the independent experiences of each converge in a universal significance that comes from a central reality. This central reality is "the life of God" and the contemplative yearns to know this universal reality in "the significant interior of life."

The problem encountered when people of different cultures approach one another is the reluctance to move from a position of superiority to one of openness and mutual respect. The way is blocked by pride and demand, and communion is frustrated. It requires a humility grounded in the contemplative experience of the life of God within, which issues in love and regard for the other. If one is in touch with the center of love within oneself, then the realization dawns that this love is present in the other, manifesting itself in creativity and freedom. The unity of love can unfold between persons who on the surface seem so different.

Merton warned against both a triumphal and close-minded Christian approach to persons of other cultures as well as any watered-down syncretism. In an amazing letter to a Nicaraguan poet, Pablo Antonio Cuadra, published in *Emblems of a Season of Fury* in 1963, Merton ruminated on matters of Western and Christian colonialism. He commented that if he was willing to give only his truth and to receive no truth back, then there could be no truth between them. But if Christ came as Word made flesh, then the fact of the incarnation implies that God can speak through any person:

> and that he can enlighten and inspire love in and through any man I meet. It is true that the visible Church alone has the official mission to sanctify and teach all nations, but no man knows that the stranger he meets coming out of the forest in a new country is not already an invisible member of Christ and perhaps one who has some providential or prophetic message to utter.[7]

What one was really trying to encounter was the truth in the person, or the true person as known in Christ. Merton was much troubled about the problem of true and false identity, as we will see when we move on to his view of spiritual direction. One of the tragedies of so-called "advanced societies," or technological societies, as he called them, is that the person is isolated as an individual to be counted and manipulated, bought and sold, quantified and made into statistics. Love is destroyed when the individual is substituted for the person, as if he or she could exist solely for personal aggrandizement and ego satisfaction apart from others. The person knows unity when he or she becomes one with love and becomes love for others and for the one source that is Love. In this way one experiences Truth.[8] We should be about seeking truth for its own sake in all people.

Spiritual direction is about finding the truth of a person's life. And that truth is discovered as the root and purpose for a person's life is discerned in the love of God unfolding in his or her life journey. Merton wrote of this ministry in a small book entitled *Spiritual Direction and Meditation.* Its purpose is to delve down beneath the surface of a person's life "to bring out his inner spiritual freedom, his inmost truth, which is what we call the likeness of Christ in his soul."[9] The true director is the Holy Spirit, and the human guide is one who helps another to follow the leadings of grace through the Spirit in her life so that she may know her vocation and come to union with God.

The model for this practice is the relationship between the "spiritual father" and the disciples who gathered around him in the ancient deserts. The disciple came to hear the words of spiritual guidance from the holy person and experienced conversion and change through "the inward action of the Holy Spirit which accompanied them, in the soul of the hearer."[10]

Thus in the relationship between two human beings the Holy Spirit makes use of the words spoken, most often simple and brief, and the hearing of those words, to affect change in an open and receptive person. The desire that paves the way for this receptivity is an eagerness to discover one's purpose for being, to embrace that truth, and to draw close to God.

Spiritual direction is the guidance of the Holy Spirit through one person who both encourages and admonishes to help another person live up to his state in life. In a series of talks on Sufism to his brother monks, Merton spoke of direction as concern to discern what is happening to a person right now: What is going on, and how does one fit it into the circumstances where he lives? It is concerned with the normal stuff of a person's life. Rather than burdening a person with "artificial patterns and the limitations of particular systems," the focus is on the lived experience of the directee.[11] What is God saying to the person right there and then? What are the promptings of grace from within in this particular situation? What are the road signs, and how does one interpret them? The essential knowledge must come from within oneself, and it is uncovered in the relationship with the director.

The director is a companion pilgrim who is concerned about the whole person. She knows that in the spiritual life a person ought to be led to a place where "in all that he does he acts freely, simply, spontaneously, from the depths of his heart, moved by love."[12] It is essentially a human relationship conducted in a friendly and unhurried atmosphere where intimate sharing can take place. The relationship is marked by trust: "The director is one who knows and sympathizes, who makes allowances, who understands circumstances, who is not in a hurry, who is patiently and humbly waiting for indications of God's action in the soul."[13]

In this relaxed and open climate, there is no agenda except to recognize that God is at work in the life of the directee and in the relationship between the two.

Traditionally spiritual direction has concerned itself with matters of prayer, personal sanctity, and spiritual discernment under the guidance of the Holy Spirit. One was expected to be obedient to her director in these matters. Today the emphasis has shifted to understand that the relationship in direction is a generative one between friends seeking out the reality of God's love and will in a person's life. Merton says that docility rather than obedience is desired, and this is a matter of prudence.[14] The deference given is based on a growing affection and trust for one who has had more experience with pilgrimage.

In matters of prayer, Merton cautioned that one can become so tangled in the methods and degrees of prayer and contemplation that the essential reason for prayer, relationship with God, can be completely forgotten. The compulsiveness of the effort to discover the right kind of prayer experience can shift the center of attention from God onto oneself. The danger of this reflexive "self-consciousness" in prayer is that "the soul turns into an opaque mirror in which the contemplative looks no longer at God but at himself."[15]

The director should be a person with an authentic prayer life who can lead the directee through such methodological self-preoccupation into a personal relationship with God, God's love, and God's will. This is the work of prayer and helps a person to become more fully human. God comes to us in and through our humanity, and it is the experienced director who can help to discern the movements of God, who both affirms and challenges in prayer.

Discernment is an essential charism in a spiritual director, a grace that is given. Merton holds that: "The value of a director lies in the clarity and simplicity of his discernment, in sound judgment, rather than in the exhortation he gives."[16] If we are willing to trust the director and to open the depths of our soul to her, then our motives can be examined and the blocks removed between our conscious self, our true self, and God.

The director can thus help in discerning whether our motives correspond to the truth and grace of God. Again this is what it means to be truly human: Not to pretend to be who we are not, whether it be a person of this or that prayer practice, or a person who adopts the human or spiritual characteristics of the director or anyone else, but rather to be a person who has been stripped of all false selves and has become fully human. True sanctity is to be found in being not less human, but rather more human.[17]

Indeed, one gives glory to God by consenting to be who he or she was created to be as a human being. In one of the most beautiful passages he ever wrote, Merton uses the metaphor of the tree:

> A tree gives glory to God by being a tree. For in being what God wants one to be it is obeying Him. It "consents," so to speak, to His creative love. It is expressing an idea which is in God and which is not distinct from the essence of God, and therefore a tree imitates God by being a tree.[18]

The question of personal identity is inextricably tied in with the identity of God. To be who I am intended to be is to conform to God's will and to imitate God. By discovering and living into the reality of my being, I "consent" to my identity, which is my "true self," and also find salvation.

The stripping away of the false self is painful, and one may be filled with dread at the realization of the lie he has been living.[19] But to be in touch with the authentic self is to find meaning for one's life and also to be freed to love. The alienated person cannot love because he is not in touch with his own authentic inner truth. He cannot love because:

> He has nothing to give. Nothing is his. The lover is able to give himself to another precisely because he is his own to give. He is not alienated. He has an identity. He knows what is his to surrender.[20]

Thus the Holy Spirit can lead us to the truth of our identity through prayer and meditation, and through the word that is discerned in the relationship of spiritual direction. This in turn enables us to love.

Merton had no doubt that love was a spiritual matter. Love is the key to both self-understanding and authentic relationships that are generative. By loving another, a person puts the other in touch with the authenticity of her own being. When a person realizes he is worthy of love, "[h]e will respond by drawing a mysterious value out of his own depths, a new identity called into being by that love which is addressed to him."[21] This love not only helps the other to discover her own truth in Christ, but also leads her to others with their many needs. She offers love to them in the compassionate works of the apostolate. Without this experience of the inner Truth, we will have nothing to give, because we are not in touch with our own true selves.

But also we will be unable to understand that which is significant in the world in which we propose to act:

Without contemplation we remain small, limited, divided, partial: we adhere to the insufficient, permanently united to our narrow group and its interests, losing sight of justice and charity, seized by the passions of the moment, and, finally, we betray Christ. Without contemplation, without the intimate silent, secret pursuit of truth through love, our action loses itself in the world and becomes dangerous.[22]

What we are asked to do is to lose ourselves in humility and to seek Christ everywhere and to find Him in everyone. Love is the ground of our being, our unity, our ministry, and our true freedom to live in relationship, which is to create. It is to find oneself bonded to all people in compassion.

As seen earlier, in order to be such agents of truth and love, we must give up our own myths of superiority. In a fascinating essay on the "Cargo Cults of the South Pacific,"[23] Merton urges those from the West to help people of other cultures to get in touch with their own authentic myth, to accept themselves on their own terms and, in a relationship of equality, to enable them to develop their own identity.

In the context of this discussion, we might think in terms of collaboration. This would call us to model candor and adaptability in our practice of spiritual direction. An expression of equality in the midst of our sharing the witness to Christ, who is our own Truth at the center, would be honest about the struggle we have to be faithful to the presence and imperative of Love within us.

If we feel that our "Western myth-dream demands of us that we spiritually enslave others in order to 'save' them,"[24] then we have no reason to be surprised when they choose to free themselves from us in order to save themselves. When we are willing to be in a relationship of humility and love, open to the direction of the Holy Spirit, sharing in love and wisdom what is the Center for us, then perhaps we can grow toward unity and peace and free ourselves of what is shallow and useless in our own pursuit of Truth.

As spiritual directors, we can do nothing better than to help others uncover their own identity and destiny as they come to know the Christ who dwells at their center. As they can claim the Truth at their center and live it in the fabric of their own lives and cultures, they are freed to engage with others in the world of peace, unity, and liberation for all peoples. Indeed, they may well help to free us from that which is distorted and oppressive in our own myth. It is not so much a question of preaching Christ at others, but prayerfully and with wonder to uncover Christ in them.

Perhaps Merton himself models for us the qualities of humility, candor, and adaptability we seek in the practice of spiritual direction. On his final journey, he met with a Tibetan spiritual master named Chatral Rimpoc in his hermitage. They discussed hermit life and shared their own experiences of prayer and solitude and found much agreement. Merton records in his journal that the Tibetan hermit had said that he had meditated for thirty years in solitude and "had not attained to perfect emptiness." Merton admitted that neither had he:

> The unspoken or half-spoken message of the talk was our complete understanding of each other as people who were somehow *on the edge* of great realization and knew it and were trying, somehow or other, to go out and get lost in it — and that it was a grace for us to meet one another.[25]

NOTES

1. Thomas Merton, *A Vow of Conversation, Journals 1964–1965* (New York: Farrar, Straus, Giroux, 1988), p. 19.

2. Thomas Merton, *Conjectures of a Guilty Bystander* (Garden City, N.Y.: Doubleday Image, 1968), p. 21.

3. "Preface to the Japanese Edition of *Seeds of Contemplation*, March 1965," as found in *Honorable Reader, Reflections on My Work*, ed. Robert E. Daggy (New York: Crossroad, 1989), p. 86.

4. "Preface to the Japanese Edition of *Thoughts in Solitude*, March 1966," as found in *Honorable Reader*, p. 112.

5. *The Asian Journal of Thomas Merton* (New York: New Directions, 1973), p. 304.

6. "Preface to the Argentine Edition of *The Complete Works of Thomas Merton*, April 1958," as found in *Honorable Reader*, p. 39.

7. *The Collected Poems of Thomas Merton* (New York: New Directions, 1977), p. 383.

8. "Preface to the Japanese Edition of *Thoughts in Solitude*," as found in *Honorable Reader*, p. 112.

9. Thomas Merton, *Spiritual Direction and Meditation* (Collegeville: Liturgical Press, 1960), p. 8.

10. Ibid., p. 5.

11. "Spiritual Direction" (Kansas City, Mo.: Credence Cassettes, 1988), tape A2213, side 2.

12. *Spiritual Direction*, p. 7.

13. Ibid., p. 25.

14. Ibid., p. 40.

15. Ibid., p. 34.

16. Ibid., p. 37.

17. Thomas Merton, *Life and Holiness* (Garden City, N.Y.: Doubleday Image, 1964), p. 24.

18. Thomas Merton, *New Seeds of Contemplation* (New York: New Directions, 1961), p. 29.

19. Thomas Merton, *Contemplative Prayer* (New York: Herder and Herder, 1969), p. 26.

20. Thomas Merton, *Contemplation in a World of Action* (Garden City, N.Y.: Doubleday, 1971), p. 71.

21. Thomas Merton, *Disputed Questions* (New York: Farrar, Straus and Cudahy, 1960), p. 125.

22. "Preface to the Argentine Edition of *The Complete Works of Thomas Merton*, April 1958," as found in *Honorable Reader*, pp. 42–43.

23. Thomas Merton, "Cargo Cults of the South Pacific," as found in *Love and Living* (New York: Farrar, Straus, Giroux, 1979), pp. 80–94.

24. Ibid., p. 94.

25. *Asian Journal*, p. 143 (Merton's emphasis).

Part II

THE PRAXIS OF CROSS-CULTURAL SPIRITUAL DIRECTION

7

Listening and Spiritual Direction in Asia

THOMAS H. O'GORMAN, SJ

For some years now it has become quite fashionable to go to the East, to Asia, to search for spiritual wisdom and guidance. Ashrams in India and Zen centers in Japan and temples in Thailand have been receiving men and women from the West by the thousands. And from Asia any number of gurus and roshis are traveling to the West, to Europe and America, to give instruction and guidance according to the religious tradition of Asia.

But what of the Westerner who goes to Asia to engage in the ministry of spiritual direction with Asians? Putting aside the issues of just what the West may have to offer the East, are there specific characteristics of spiritual direction in Asia that challenge the Western man or woman as a spiritual director? This is the focus of this essay.

Of course there are any number of aspects of spiritual direction that might be considered. But because listening is such a central element in spiritual direction, and because listening in a cross-cultural context can be rather mysterious and perplexing, this essay addresses itself to listening in spiritual direction from an Asian perspective. The spiritual director in Asia, as elsewhere, wants to listen to God as well as to the Asian directee who seeks direction.[1] The spiritual director in Asia will also want to listen to Asia itself, or at least to that part of Asia in which the directee is engaged. Listening to God is not particularly specific to Asia. But insofar as God reveals God's self in a specific way in the Asian context, listening to an Asian directee may call for attention to particular factors and to particular dynamics of interpersonal communication.

Is there an experienced spiritual guide today who does not place a very high value on the art of listening as a major requirement for the ministry of spiritual direction? A constant concern of any director is to listen in such a way that there is an adequate understanding of what is being communicated, since there is no genuine spiritual direction without sufficiently clear communication. How discouraging it can be for a director to be told, "I am sorry, but I do not think you have understood what I have been telling you; perhaps you have not been listening to me."

The most commonly accepted vehicle for communication in spiritual direction is the one-to-one conversation that takes place between the persons involved.[2] Obviously this is a conversation that gives priority to an open and accepting listening on the part of the director, a listening to the other's disclosure of what is being intimately experienced in a personal relationship with God. The director tries to listen to what the directee discloses about how he or she finds the revelation of God interiorly and in the myriad situations and events of life. To be sure, spiritual direction cannot be limited to simply listening, but listening is a starting point and remains a necessary element throughout the direction process.

The listening that is at issue is a listening that pays attention to far more than mere words. The experience of God and of God's dealings within us cannot be adequately expressed by a language that is limited to words. Hence we have long been cautioned not to neglect the many nonverbal signs that help us communicate what we experience within the depth of our being. A spiritual director today will hopefully be aware that effective listening requires an attentiveness to structures of personal communication that vary from person to person. Often enough the director who is being told that he or she has not heard or understood what has been said is being told that he or she has not paid sufficient attention to the nonverbal or, to coin a term, the "extra-verbal" communication of the directee.

As a director I must of course listen to words and try to understand what they convey, but I listen to much more than words. I also listen to silence and try to understand what this means, too. Tears and laughter, with all of the ambiguity involved, must be heard with as much understanding as possible. Our bodies speak with gestures and movements that can reveal far more than words can reveal. And quite hidden among these nonverbals is the whole set of social structures and circumstances that make up a directee's environment and also need to be heard. What are some of the "extra-verbals" that a director in Asia will find herself listening to? What are some of the Asian realities that a director will want to attend to, so as to listen to Asian directees?

But first, some preliminary assumptions should be stated. In the setting of spiritual direction, the director is listening to a particular person, not to some imaginary ideal. That means that the director desires to listen to this particular person with an understanding of his or her particular background, perceiving as much as possible the various forces that contribute to identify and particularize this person. These forces can be social, economic, cultural, physical—all the elements of this person's background.

Each one of us has been formed through structures of family relationships, by education (both formal and nonformal). We have been trained, often unconsciously, to relate with one another according to well-established patterns of social communication. To the very roots of our being, we are affected by that mysterious thing called "culture." The more my spiritual director knows and understands the many constitutive forces in my life that make me who and what I am, the more will that director be able to "listen" to me when I relate my inner experiences and when I describe how I experience God in my life. In any situation of spiritual direction, the listening of the director will necessarily be, therefore, a "contextual" listening. The listening that is involved in spiritual direction in Asia will have to be a listening that takes into consideration particularly Asian factors.

DIVERSITY IN THE ASIAN SCENE

But is it possible to make generalizations in a discussion of Asian factors? At this point a few observations about Asia and Asians may be in order to set the stage for further reflections.

There may have been a time when people of the Western world looked upon Asia as part of a great mystery, and quite possibly a mystery that was viewed in a rather simplistic way. In the past there was an abundance of stereotypes that identified Asians with the sketches of Rudyard Kipling's tales or with characters in "The Mikado" of Gilbert and Sullivan. As so often happens, the challenge of Asia's depths was frequently met with an oversimplification through caricatures that unwittingly tried to do away with the mystery.

Today, however, the reality of Asia is finding an entry into our world consciousness that breaks the stereotypes of the past. One can imagine Asia as a giant that is stirring out of long years of enforced slumber, and now the rest of the world is beginning to be aware of Asia in a new and hopefully more perceptive way.

To describe Asia without oversimplifications is not easy, because the Asian reality is so diverse. To begin with, the geographic description of Asia is somewhat problematic. Is it realistic to contain in one set of boundaries an area that stretches from the northern islands of Japan to the southern shores of Indonesia and from the eastern islands of the Philippine archipelago to the western limits of the vast Indian subcontinent? Include within this territory the regions of today's eastern and northern Russia, as well as the areas described by Afghanistan and Pakistan, and the Asian giant appears even more immense.[3] An area of the globe that contains about 60 percent of the world's population cannot be expected to be a center of uniformity!

Geographical diversity, however, is not the only nor the most important consideration. Symptomatic of how different one Asian can be from another are the cultural differences that abound within this whole called Asia, even within individual Asian countries, and the cultural conflicts that are erupting throughout this continent as the last decade of the twentieth century gets underway. Is it possible to speak of a typical Asian in any meaningful way?

Political history has not dealt well with Asia, and a sad legacy of much of the colonization within the area has been the formation of quite a number of artificial national boundaries on the one hand, and on the other, a retardation of real national identity for many of today's so-called emerging nations in the region.[4] Not unconnected to Asia's political development is its very uneven economic development. One can witness within Asia very great extremes of poverty and wealth, with all of the weakening effects that both excessive wealth and intense poverty have on individuals, peoples, and nations.

Those who believe in one God may hope to find in religion an element that unifies Asia to some degree, but the fact is that at present religious Asia, the home of some of the world's "great religions," is deeply divided. Islam, Hinduism, Buddhism were born in Asia and remain powerfully alive throughout the region. Of more local significance are Chinese Taoism, Japanese Shintoism, and Korean Shamanism, religions that are experiencing at once both decline and determined efforts at revival. Affecting the practice of religion while not religion in itself is Confucianism. And to round out the picture, mention should be made of the many animistic religions.[5] Into this Asian religious world Christianity has been introduced from "outside," with its own problems of disunity and frequent identification with foreign colonizing or conquering "powers."

Now to return to spiritual direction and the listening it requires, particularly in the Asian context. In any situation it is necessary for the spiritual director to know how to communicate with the person being guided, how to listen to what is being communicated. As noted above, the more the director knows of the person, what lies behind and underneath the appearances, what is rooted deeply within the person, the better is the director able to really listen and to interpret the signs of communication. What are some of the specifics of this listening in today's Asian context? Three areas will be discussed here: the director–directee relationship in Asian settings, some Asian ways of prayer, challenges in the Asian social condition.

DIRECTOR–DIRECTEE RELATIONSHIP

Characteristic of many Asian cultures, especially those that are influenced by Confucian traditions, is the great reverence and respect given to elders and to those perceived to be in positions of authority. Often the spiritual director will be placed unconsciously in an authority position. If this happens, it is not unlikely that the directee will say to the director whatever it seems the director would like to hear—what would be pleasing to the director.

Does this mean that the directee is being deceitful? One might be tempted to think so, but some cultures might see things differently. Quite possibly it may not be deceit but rather an effort to give a respectful response to something that the director may have already expressed (albeit nonverbally), namely that such a response is desired. In other words, in the communication that is taking place the director has already "said" nonverbally to the person being guided, "What I hope you will say to me is . . . "[6] The directee here is responding to the director according to certain expectations that are being very subtly communicated by the director. Naturally the difficulty is increased if the director actually does give the impression of being disappointed or displeased with what the directee discloses or reports.

The natural respect with which many Asians will want to deal with a spiritual director will also affect much of the nonverbal communication. Body language is an important case in point. While among Westerners lack of eye contact might be interpreted as a sign that something significant is being held back, it might not be so with an Asian. A reluctance to look the director in the eye may be an expression of respect and not at all a sign that the directee is not open. A director's insistence that a directee "be relaxed" (with bodily positions that speak of relaxation to a Westerner) may, in the Asian context, produce more tension than relaxation. Even with body language, the director must be careful not to misinterpret the communication and try to force something that will be artificial.

Somewhat akin to the almost automatic stance of respect toward the director that may be the outcome of Confucian traditions is the reluctance to engage in personal confrontation or disagreement with a friend. In many Asian cultures a high value is placed on maintaining good and smooth relationships among friends, and confrontation—even at times disagreement over issues—is often considered to be too risky for a friendship to bear. Of course there are situations when confrontations do erupt, and with surprising violence (the level of violence may in fact be in proportion to the level of repressed disagreement), but the spiritual direction situation is not one where such eruptions are usually helpful. On the contrary, it is the usual understanding that the relationship involved in spiritual direction is a positive one, a relationship that is friendly.[7] As a matter of fact, once a relationship has been hurt by a violent confrontation, it is frequently very difficult to repair it without great loss of self-esteem.[8] Here again the spiritual director must be alert to the subjective position of the person being guided. Obviously the more free that person is and the more that person feels at ease, the more likely it is that there will be a clear flow of communication.

From what has been said so far it should be obvious that in a cross-cultural setting extra attention must be given to developing clarity of understanding in the communication between director and directee. While it may be very true that the directee will have to be trained to communicate clearly to this director, the main burden is on the director to adjust to the communication style of the directee. While Asian directees may be as inarticulate as any others when it comes to communicating interior experiences and feelings, a good director will be aware of the many dynamics that can enter into a direction conversation.[9] A lack of an understanding awareness here can result in confused communication.

Quite obviously the time and effort spent in clarifying the relationship between this director and this directee is time and effort well invested. The director should have a sense of how he or she is perceived by the directee: as an authority figure or guru to be obeyed; as a friend whose friendship must not be lost or weakened by disagreement; as an elder who must be respected with an attitude of compliance?[10] It is not so much a question of how the director sees himself or herself, but of how the director is perceived by the directee. And although the principal relationship to be concerned about is that between the directee and God, nevertheless the quality of the relationship between the director and the directee will greatly affect the way in which the principal God-relationship is influenced by the communication process within spiritual direction.

In some particular Asian contexts, a non-native spiritual director may be at a disadvantage from the very beginning of the spiritual direction relationship. It was pointed out above that the political history of Asia has left its mark, and like it or not, a spiritual director who is a foreigner may be seen to represent, even if symbolically, an oppressive colonizing power. Not infrequently what is considered by the Westerner as a free, open, honest, and frank approach to a directee will be perceived to be overly aggressive and domineering, if not oppressive. This may be particularly so if the directee comes from a background of a national struggle for independence from Western control and dominance.

ASIAN WAYS OF PRAYER

Although prayer is not the only matter for reflection in spiritual direction, how one prays and how one experiences God in prayer will be the focus of much of the conversation between the director and the directee. Recently expressed concerns about so-called Eastern prayer and Eastern ways of prayer highlight the importance of the attention that a spiritual director in Asia gives to prayer and the ways of prayer.[11] As a matter of fact, many in Asia have found that their ordinary way of prayer is prayer in the Eastern mode, prayer highly conceptual and so often apparently without content. Throughout Asia today, as indeed in other parts of the world, Christians are being taught to pray according to what have been called Eastern methods, styles that often borrow heavily from Buddhist traditions.[12]

In their second plenary assembly, the bishops of the Federation of Asian Bishops' Conferences recognized the contribution that the great religions of Asia can make to the Church and recognized the value in the prayer traditions of Asia.[13] Whether or not the actual integration of Eastern prayer methods is appropriate or successful in a particular instance may be a matter for discernment, but in Asia today a spiritual director should have a sufficiently sympathetic and well-informed understanding of prayer in the Asian traditions of the directees who are seeking to respond more freely and faithfully to God as God calls them.

Many who pray according to Eastern methods are finding that there is much truth underlying the Second Vatican Council's words to religious missionary institutes in its decree on missionary activity:

> Let them reflect attentively on how Christian religious life may be able to assimilate the ascetic and contemplative traditions whose seeds were some-times already planted by God in various cultures prior to the preaching of the Gospel.[14]

It would be unfortunate for a spiritual director to judge that noncon-ceptual prayer, or prayer apparently without content, is not Christian. At the heart of prayer is God's communication with us and not our thoughts about God. And it is not foreign to the Christian tradition to recognize God as ineffable. It would be a mistake to judge automatically that for a praying Christian the "nothingness" or the "emptiness" of many forms of Eastern prayer refers to a nonexistence or even to an absence of God. Quite the contrary may be true: In the "no-thing-ness" the Absolute who cannot be expressed adequately by rational words and concepts is contem-plated and is allowed to be present. In our communication with God in prayer, we who are in Christ by the power of the Spirit (to call on the theology of Paul) should not be surprised that we do not need words or concepts so that we can experience God.[15]

In the whole effort to promote genuine inculturation in Asia, its impor-tance in the area of prayer cannot be neglected. The point here is not that the spiritual director will necessarily be responsible for introducing direc-tees to traditionally Asian ways of prayer. As a matter of fact, a spiritual director who would force Eastern prayer methods on directees for whom these forms are not their way of prayer could be doing a great disservice. It must be admitted that for many, if not for most Christians in Asia, the prayer methods of the traditional "great religions" are actually not the usual ways of praying. But a spiritual director in Asia today should be able to give suitable guidance to a directee whose prayer is so inculturated. If a particular director finds that he or she is incapable of this, the best path may be for that director to suggest someone else for the task.[16]

Much of the attention given to prayer according to Eastern methods is attention to Hindu and Buddhist methods. But as has been pointed out above, it is inaccurate to identify Hinduism or Buddhism with all that is Asian. Particularly in Southeast Asia, we can find very different characteristics. In contrast to the quiet and stillness that is typical of many northern and western Asians, we find an abundance of sound and action. Instead of the absence of images, we can find a plethora of images and religious symbols.[17] Dance, song, and vibrant voice (often in some form of group prayer) reflect the natural way of communicating with God for many Asians who are not of the Hindu or Buddhist traditions. Without denying the need for quiet and stillness, a spiritual director should be alert to the need to integrate such prayer into the direction process. This is also part of the task of listening in the Asian context.

ASIAN SOCIAL CONDITIONS

These considerations of prayer and the spiritual direction conversation began with an almost parenthetical observation that prayer is not the only focus in spiritual direction. In vast parts of Asia today, God's word is heard in social situations of dire poverty and injustice. It is difficult to see how a spiritual director can be faithful to the ministry of facilitating the relationship between God and individuals if attention is not given to how God speaks in Asia to Asians about injustice and poverty. Again it may be that the first task of the director will be to listen to silence, to be aware of what might be called a deafness to God's word. But listen the director must, not only to the directee but also to the social situation. If the director is not aware of the objective social situation of injustice and poverty in Asia, and if the directee is likewise unaware of the same, the spiritual direction conversation may well be a case of the deaf leading the deaf, to say nothing of the blind leading the blind.[18] It is presumed here that we accept the challenge to be a Church of the poor, a challenge that is particularly urgent for Asia.

In this regard, a spiritual director in Asia should be aware of the passion for justice that many Asian directees will bring to spiritual direction. Here there is a crying need for discernment that is genuinely Christian, as men and women in many countries of Asia today try to discover just what their response to God should be in the face of a wide variety of ideologies that are often in subtle, if not open conflict, among themselves and with Christianity. It will be important for a director to be aware of his or her own ideology as well as of the ideologies that may be exercising an influence on the directee.

Some directors may object that entering into this field is straying a bit far from the primary responsibility of spiritual direction.[19] The focus of spiritual direction, one may rightly insist, is the directee's experience of God. True, but the experience of God as God present in the social situation in which we live should have much to say to both the director and the directee. This God, who calls out to us in the cry of the poor and oppressed around us, is not a different God from the God who speaks in the "privacy" of our felt inner movements. Of course, the director must be very careful not to take the place of God, but helping a directee to become aware of God's presence and call does not seem to be contrary to the director's "proper task to facilitate discovery" and to help "individuals freely to place themselves before God who will communicate himself to them and make them more free."[20]

Certainly in most of Asia, as in so many other parts of the Third World, God is calling us to a spirituality of greater social awareness than many of us may have suspected in the past.[21] Spiritual direction that does not listen to this calling God, even in the silence of unawareness in the directee, runs the risk of becoming a direction that may be called spiritualistic but which is not truly spiritual. An irony is that a director who studiously avoids entering into this area so as to be faithful to God as God is, may actually be creating a god who is not real; instead of listening to the real God, this director may be listening to a limited and false god. Rather than leading a directee to greater freedom, the director may be setting limits to the freedom to which God is calling the person.

CONCLUSION

In any ongoing dialogue of spiritual direction, there is much listening to be done. The directee is, in a sense, the first listener, listening to God's call "heard" within the total context of that person's experience of God. The director will want to help and facilitate the directee's listening, but in doing so, he or she will have to be a careful listener. For the Western director in Asia, this will often mean learning a new "language" and understanding new dynamics of personal communication. It will frequently mean growing in an awareness of one's own "filters" in order not to misinterpret what is said and what may be left unsaid. It will also mean that the director will have to grow in an understanding (to be sure, a sympathetic understanding) of this particular directee's Asian way of communicating with God in prayer. Together with the directee, the director in Asia will be challenged to listen to God speaking and crying out in a world of poverty and injustice.

All of this listening is for the sake of responding, so that our Christian response to God will be a faithful one. The director in Asia, as elsewhere, is engaged in a helping ministry that listens to God, in Christ, who proclaims again in today's world:

> The spirit of the Lord is upon me;
>   therefore, He has anointed me.
> He has sent me to bring glad tidings to the poor,
>   to proclaim liberty to captives,
> Recovery of sight to the blind
>   and release to prisoners,
> To announce a year of favor from the Lord.
>   Luke 4:18–19

NOTES

1. The term *directee* is not a happy one, but it will be used here for want of any word that can better describe the Christian who seeks to be guided by another in the living out of his or her relationship with God. The spiritual direction envisioned here is the direction of Christians that is ongoing and therefore by no means limited to the somewhat specific situation of direction during the time of a retreat.

2. *See* William A. Barry and William J. Connolly, *The Practice of Spiritual Direction* (New York: The Seabury Press, 1982), p. 11. It is presumed that the spiritual direction discussed here is that of mature adults, not that of novices or situations where instruction is the main concern. For a discussion of the various "models" of spiritual direction, *see* David L. Fleming, "Models of Spiritual Direction," *Review for Religious* 34 (1974): 351–57.

3. A good and readable summary presentation of the complexity of Asia can be found in Generoso M. Flórez, SJ, *An Appeal to the Church: The Mission of the Church in Asia* (Anand, India: Gujarat Sahitya Prakash, 1986), pp. 10–37. Here Flórez remarks: "It was only the audacity of European cartographers that put together the homelands of the Arab, Persian, Turkish, Indian, Chinese and South-East civilizations and gave them the name 'Asia.' "

4. An example of artificial boundaries is that of the border between Papua New Guinea and Indonesia in Irian Java. There is also artificiality in the national boundaries of what was once called "Indochina." Examples of the retardation of Asian national identity are seen in the continued economic dependence of many Asian countries on their former colonizers. Into this category falls the Philippines, with its heavy reliance on the United States.

5. Flórez, *An Appeal to the Church*, pp. 22–37, provides an overview of the religious diversity in Asia. It should be pointed out that although many adherents of the various religions do not faithfully practice their religion, the background influence of religious traditions can be quite strong.

6. Guidebooks often warn tourists in many Asian countries to be slow to take at face value such simple answers as "yes" and "no" when the desire to please is involved. Advice to tourists can be advice to spiritual directors for obviously more important reasons.

7. Today a number of authors stress the friendship dimension of the spiritual direction relationship. Patrick Purnell, in "Spiritual Direction as a Process," *The Way Supplement* 54 (Autumn 1984): 3, writes: "The relationship between director and dirigé is rooted in Christian friendship." But he goes on to point out: "Nevertheless, the dirigé comes to the director, and the latter, therefore, plays the leading role in the relationship and lays down the ground plan of the relationship." If this is so, one can see the pressures that may be unknowingly placed on the Asian "dirigé" to at once respect the "authority" of the director and carefully maintain the friendship involved. The director may well be placed quite unknowingly in the unwelcome position of a potential manipulator. *See* Leonard Schwatzburd, Ph.D., "The Risky Confrontation of Friends," *Human Development* 9 (Summer 1988): 27–30, where the problematics of dealing with the "risks" may speak more directly to a Western context than to an Asian one.

8. It is interesting to observe the role of a mediator or a "go-between" in the process of restoring damaged personal relationships in a number of Asian cultures.

An unfair, but common characterization of Asian patterns of relationships is that the Asian more than others must "save face." Usually this is understood by Westerners in a pejorative sense. The level of concern in the West for developing a positive self-image should tell us something about the universality of being uncomfortable with the harm done through a lack of positive self-esteem.

9. Keeping in mind Asian specifics, *see* Barry and Connolly, pp. 65–79, for their treatment of how to develop the ability to articulate deep inner feelings and attitudes.

10. This is particularly true if the director does actually hold a position of some authority, such as that of an appointed director of a formation program, a retreat director, or even simply a person considered to be an "expert" in spiritual direction.

11. See the "Letter to the Bishops of the Catholic Church on Some Aspects of Christian Meditation" of the Congregation for the Doctrine of the Faith, *L'Osservatore Romano* (English weekly edition), 2 January 1990: 8–10, 12. The highly cautionary tone of this instruction may lead many to suspect that its authors do not sufficiently understand how Eastern ways of praying have been genuinely helpful for many Asian Christians. It is feared that, as often appears to be the case with Vatican documents, the need to correct and caution is exaggerated while the value of encouraging and supporting does not get the appreciation it deserves.

12. The question of bringing together Ignatian spirituality (especially for Jesuits in their formative years) and Asian ways of prayer was addressed in a seminar that was held in Manila in 1983 at the East Asian Pastoral Institute. The papers presented at that seminar can be found in *Asian Forms of Prayer: A Pastoral Seminar* published in Manila in 1983 by the Jesuit Conference of East Asia. Some of the papers were also published as "A Pastoral Seminar on Asian Forms of Prayer," *East Asian Pastoral Review* 20 (1983): 338–62. The success and popularity of the work that had been done by Fr. Anthony de Mello, SJ, is testimony to the widespread acceptance of Eastern influences. *See* his *Sadhana: A Way to God*, 5th ed. (Amand, India: Gujarat Sahitya Prakash, 1981).

13. *See* the final statement of the FABC's Second Plenary Assembly, "Prayer: The Life of the Church of Asia," in *For All the Peoples of Asia*, vol. 1 (Manila: IMC Publications, 1984), pp. 49–74. *See also* the workshop discussion guides for that same plenary assembly, "Prayer, Community Worship and Inculturation," *FABC Papers*, no. 12.

14. *Ad Gentes*, no. 18, in *The Documents of Vatican II*, ed. Walter M. Abbott, SJ (New York: America Press, 1966), p. 607.

15. For an account of one person's spiritual journey with Eastern prayer and his efforts at an integration with Ignatian spirituality, *see* Daniel J. O'Hanlon, SJ, "Integration of Christian Practices: A Western Christian Looks East," *Studies in the Spirituality of Jesuits* 16 (May 1984): 1–27.

16. In any context, referral from one director to another can be delicate and the decision to "change directors" must be carefully made and communicated. In Asia a director should be extra careful not to give the directee the impression of being rejected.

17. Much more serious attention is being given today than in the past to what has often been called "folk religiosity" and branded as superstition.

18. A personal conviction of this author is that it is important for spiritual directors in Asia to have both lived experience and some reflected understanding (with the help of the tools of the social sciences, such as social analysis) of the

social, political, and economic situations of Asia. Otherwise, the spirituality fostered in direction is in danger of being unreal and unresponsive to God's call today.

19. *See*, for example, the remarks of Barry and Connolly (pp. 43–44), which some may want to interpret in a way supportive of this objection. While it may be wise not to pursue this social dimension of God's call in situations of certain retreats (although that also may be questioned), our discussion of spiritual direction here is not limited to the direction that takes place during a retreat. On this topic, a lively discussion between Jesuits Philip S. Land and William J. Connolly can be found in "Jesuit Spiritualities and the Struggle for Social Justice," *Studies in the Spirituality of Jesuits* 9 (September 1977). Though the actual discussion in these pages may now seem somewhat dated, the issues raised are still very much alive.

20. Barry and Connolly, p. 44.

21. Concern for social conditions of poverty and injustice are surely not to be limited to the Third World, but the fact is that the urgency of a discerning social consciousness is experienced more acutely in the Third World.

8

Experiences of the Heart:
The Spiritual Exercises across Cultures

LILY QUINTOS, rc

There is a well-known saying that Asians think with their hearts. The validity of this saying becomes evident as one journeys with them through the Spiritual Exercises of St. Ignatius.

In this article, I will attempt to share my own experience of directing persons from the diverse cultures of the world. I will limit my observations to Asians, to whom I have had the joy of giving the Spiritual Exercises in either the complete form of at least one month or adapted forms of varying lengths. Many of these retreatants come to the experience of the Spiritual Exercises of St. Ignatius with a rich cultural heritage that may have been influenced by Buddhism, Confucianism, and Taoism. Inevitably these cultural backgrounds will play an important part in the mode of receiving the Exercises, even though there is no conscious reference to these religious currents. The following account, however, must not be taken as empirical data. These are my own personal observations of persons who have experienced intense and intimate relations with God while under my direction.

Asia is a geographical location, and I must caution that the word *Asia* is not used to indicate a single entity but as the mix of different cultures that it is. As a continent, Asia is rich in diverse traditions. Peoples of Asia do not have a sense of common descent, but rather claim different root civilizations.

Buddhism, Confucianism, and Taoism are the three most powerful currents of culture in Asia, especially in China, Korea, Japan, Taiwan, and Vietnam. Regardless of the fact that new ways of life and religious patterns have been adopted, the pervasive influence of these three systems continues to shape aspirations, fears, preferences, prejudices, and perceptions of indi-

89

viduals as they do for the arts, literature, religion, government, and the different social and civic institutions in Asia. As Jungian psychologists point out, these three currents of Eastern culture constitute, and continue to form and re-form, the "collective unconscious" of Asians at ever deeper levels.

Awareness of differences in perception of these currents in the memories of people will help the spiritual director catch delicate distinctions that may at first seem inconsequential. When distinctions are recognized as part of a larger pattern, it is possible to discern that there is a definite route being followed in the spiritual journey. Knowledge of the different philosophical or religious premises and perceptions helps the director be sensitive to what underlies religious behavior patterns in a clear, differentiated context.

The values people hold and the aspirations and goals they seek are found in the subtlety of their cultures as well as their personal drives for self-fulfillment. Culture is a powerful factor in determining modes of behavior as well as spiritual development, and the spiritual director must treat seriously the nuances in spiritual behavior patterns that may seem only trivial at times but are in fact crucial to spiritual discernment.

I will now look at my experience of directing Asian people during the first week of the Spiritual Exercises. It is always a delight to recognize how certain elements of the Exercises could be related to Buddhism, Confucianism, and Taoism. The retreatants themselves were not consciously making these connections, but this relationship was quite evident as different directees told me their experiences in prayer.

One of the functions of the spiritual director is to lead the directee in the way of integration. From a cross-cultural perspective, Asian directees in general seem to arrive at the goal quite quickly because of the "built-in" holistic approach to reality and spirituality. They are less besieged by complications and experience the process of integration as normal. In most cases, therefore, when presented with the unified worldview in the "Principle and Foundation" of the Exercises, they resonate and reflect a similar unified worldview, but with a slightly nuanced, personal touch. For them, a unified view of the world means that the wholeness of creation can be found not simply by "adjusting" to external reality, but more importantly, by responding to one's deepest and most natural intuitions and inclinations as a creature of God, of being oneself in God and with and through others.

I recall one of my directees paraphrasing the "Principle and Foundation" something like this:

> The one true accomplishment on earth is escape from the prison of my own self. Most things created bring suffering, pain and hurt; their most subtle consequence is to leave one dulled to the hurt they cause. Unlike other parts of creation, persons must be more their natural selves because we are heaven-endowed; therefore we are called to be saints. Salvation itself is a problem because my own freedom complicates the process. This self, who is trying to

be a real self, at one with her God, is actually an illusion. As a consequence, one is unable to recognize what is real. The presumption is that reality is the self with all its drives and desires. But if I want to find myself, I must find God first.

This paraphrase of one retreatant's reaction echoes the reactions of a number of retreatants.

The Ignatian understanding of "indifference" is well received by retreatants coming from the Buddhist-influenced culture, and they readily accept the concept. As they apply this concept to their prayer, comparable Buddhist teachings surface. The root cause of suffering, according to Buddhist tradition, is enslavement to desire, inordinate attachments, and absorption of the self. The self, after all, is an illusion. The need then is detachment from a tenacious desire of the self to assert both the self and the desire. It is interesting to note in this context that retreatants with Buddhist backgrounds find difficulty in the words so often used in the Exercises, such as, "If I find what I desire ... " or " ... ask for what I *desire.*"

During the first week of the Spiritual Exercises, retreatants are led to face themselves as they are before God. In this process of arriving at the realization that the real self is the one who is in open communication with God, retreatants experience difficulty reconciling both the notions that they are loved and that they are "illusions." How can God love an illusion? Retreatants do not express the difficulty in these terms, but the difficulty is nonetheless in the back of their minds: the impermanent, illusory nature of the self that is called to a relationship with the Eternal God. Attempts to reconcile these contrasting notions through reason are often experienced as futile and fruitless, because the reality is not grasped by reason but encountered in contemplation.

Asian emphasis on finding meaning from experience and not from thinking, and the belief that the search for meaning is not for the individual self in isolation but in the context of community, seem to be very much in evidence in the approach to spiritual development. Buddhism, for example, starts with the process of transformation from within through personal reflection on one's experience, and works at breaking down personal barriers which reinforce illusion. No amount of doctrinal teaching leads to conversion; conversion can only be effected by the impact of values incarnate in living witnesses.

For example, the Ignatian "tantum quantum" rule is read in the light of the directee's own experience of power and possession as transitory. Directees perceive values that grow out of their understanding of the thrust for goodness which they experience from within. These values then take on concrete shape and form in the behaviors evidenced in interaction with others. Experience, in the Buddhist view, is a specific way of testing this interior experience of goodness within the complex and often conflict-ridden exchanges that compromise human social existence. This kind of experiential knowing, which touches the experience of goodness within, is the basis and measure of the progress of the spiritual life. Because it is the "experience of the heart" that is being communicated to the director, interactions between the director and the directee become less cerebral, less abstract, and consequently more fruitful. What comes to light is the existential, experiential goodness evidenced in external relationships. Such sharing enables the director to sense the pulse and movement of the directee's spiritual life.

In terms of the overall view of the "principle and foundation" for persons of Buddhist background, the particular values and criteria for action are dictated by their understanding of a unified and final goal. Buddhists' beliefs in the importance of experience and the riches of their own ancient spiritual traditions are clarified and concretized in the way in which they internalize religious and psychological perspectives as they enter into the Spiritual Exercises. The meetings of the two systems, the Christian and the Buddhist, can help the retreatant go beyond any biased, limited, or contrived explanations and focus rather on those most fundamental decisions and insights that ground any person's life. This then can lead to a greater, more pervasive experience of a fundamental faith rooted in this Buddhist experience of a unified, final goal and the Christian experience of Jesus Christ as Savior, the final, unique revelation of God.

One constant preoccupation that recurs in the course of the first week of retreat for Buddhist-influenced retreatants is whether their dedication and effort is real discipline. They wonder whether the method is leading them to the wisdom and fruit intended for that week in the Exercises. I suspect that this is due to the years of discipline they have experienced in "The Path," which tells them that no one can attain anything in the spiritual life without such discipline.

The questions most frequently raised are: If Christian belief affirms that the self is good, then why is there a need to keep striving toward that good? If Christ has redeemed us, then why the experience of being unredeemed? Why does the journey toward wholeness seem endless? These questions preoccupy Westerners as well as Easterners.

My observation is that for persons whose culture is other than Western, and especially for those in the Confucian-influenced culture, the belief in the innate goodness of human nature is reinforced because, in fact, innate goodness is an ontological assertion in their tradition. Therefore they can quite easily see the goal of making this assertion an existential lived reality. Followers of Confucius consider the self as a transcendent reference point. Ontologically, the original nature of the self is heaven-endowed and oriented. It is "divine" in all its fullness. Translated into the language of the Spiritual Exercises, the concept can be expressed in terms of God endowing every person with tremendous gifts and also bestowing on them the potentiality, the capacity, to fulfill those gifts and become fully who God intends them to be. Grace builds on nature, and human nature, in its pristine originality, is "capable of God" (*capax Dei*). Of course, the Confucian ideal does not consider "grace" as relevant to self-fulfillment.

In the teachings of Confucius, the structure of the self is such that the longing for the transcendent is extremely powerful. However, there is a fine nuance to the understanding of the human beings' "transcendence toward God." This yearning for the transcendent is not toward an "Other" Supreme Being but for the heaven that has gifted them with their original nature. But in its deepest expression the longing for the transcendent is the desire to go beyond the self. Confucian-influenced cultures consider the fulfillment of the self in and through social relationships as their "ultimate concern."

A Chinese person once explained that the word *person*, when written, has two characters—the character for "man" and the character for "two," because a person is defined by the relationship between persons. The "heaven-endowed nature" is appropriated through relationships. A good relationship with one's father is virtually one's salvation, and without it the goal of wholeness cannot be achieved. Even though social relationships are not the ultimate goal of one's existence, they nevertheless play a vital part in Confucian symbolism, since they connect so deeply with one's psyche and encompass one's religious quest.

The father-child relationship provides a context for spiritual growth. In cases where there is a difficulty in father-child relationships, the transition from a belief in a God/Creator who endows every person with gifts can sometimes be difficult and can block authentic encounter with a loving God. When directees feel that they are relating to God as father or Creator, and when they experience their own personal creaturehood, probably they have unconsciously made the connection between the Confucian "heaven-endowed nature" and the biological father to God the Father who endows the person with spiritual, personal gifts.

Although the Confucian view of the self prescinds any notion of sin and grace in the Christian sense, Confucians are quick to recognize the presence of personal frailty and proneness to evil. This awareness of the difficulties raised by personal or communal propensity to evil prompts Confucians to see spiritual growth as a communal achievement rather than a result of their own personal, individual efforts. However, the search for meaning, whether Buddhist, Confucian, or Christian, is not for the individual self but for the individual in a communal context. In other words, people do not exist for themselves but for others. In Confucian-influenced culture, the word *sin* is never used to describe guilt experienced as a consequence of wrong done. Only the behavior that is harmful to another whom one loves and especially on whom one depends is considered guilt evoking. In most cases the experience of guilt is largely due to the failure to perform well as a daughter or a son or as an employee. It is in these failures that we are to understand the meaning of social and personal transgressions. Such failure can result in the development of a "punitive conscience" where aggression is directed against the self. In addition, it is this, what one might call "potential to guilt," that determines most often their drive to be successful and influences much of their behavior.

In this context, I have noted that the Ignatian "repetition" can be easily misconstrued by the directee as a sign of failure, even though the director explains at length its meaning and purpose. Rather than use the word *repetition*, it is simpler to say, "Return to those points where you have experienced God in a very personal, meaningful way." Or "Turn to those points where you have experienced significant movements of the Spirit and allow God's revelation to unfold in more profound ways for you." In several cases where this approach was used, there was a marked difference in the directees' approach to prayer, and their sharing of their personal experience went something like this:

> In praying over my sin history, I asked God for the grace of deeper awareness of the effects of these sins in my life. At first, I did not get much out of prayer but I was also unaware of any resistance on my part. I returned to the same material for prayer and I sensed that God wishes to show me more.

When I listen to directees expressing the guilt they have felt, the experience of struggle and frustration, I do not find a rearticulation of the emotional reactions back to them, as in nondirective counseling situations, to be a method that is very useful. It seems to ground them in the vicious circle of the trauma rather than move them forward. I find that a discreet use of Annotations 7 and 8[1] is more effective in helping them move forward. I find that by waiting, laying the groundwork for the Spirit to breathe where it wills, the real issue surfaces and directees recognize it for what it is. It is important for directors to be alert in order to discern and recognize it, since the issue in question is likely to surface during prayer. Sometimes because of the lack of an understanding of what it entails to be influenced by a particular culture it is possible for a director to miss the actual structure of guilt in the directee's personality.

Another observation worthy of note regarding the experience of guilt has to do with individuals' resentful, often hostile, feelings toward their parents. Many explain this in terms of shame-oriented culture. Yet studies have shown that when a Japanese person, for example, expresses worthlessness, it is very possible that there are unresolved aggressive feelings toward loved ones that in Confucian-influenced cultures is what constitutes worthlessness. What is more readily explained as shame is actually a propensity toward devaluation of the self. When directees are given passages from Scripture to contemplate, those passages that fill them with God's presence and reaffirm God's unconditional love seem helpful. Retreatants often do a "repetition" of those passages until they feel that deep pool of certainty within that God loves them.

From the Taoist perspective, the "sin" experience is the deviation from the three fundamental principles known as Tao, Te, and Wu-wei. The Taoist "sin" is to go against the Way (Tao) by deviating from the natural course of things for one's personal benefit. Tao is also the harmony in the universe that blends all events and each moment into one perfect whole. Each movement synchronizes with the whole, the Tao. To be in harmony, in accord with Tao, is to be in a state of Te, also known in Christian terms as "grace," "virtue," or "power." Te is best understood as Tao actualized in the human person.

Tao and Te are operative under the principle of Wu-wei, which unites them. Harmony is achieved through the action of Wu-wei. Any use of force is considered a symptom of weakness and leads to failure. The *"agere contra"* of St. Ignatius (going against the natural inclination to evil that is the consequence of the Fall) needs to be interpreted in the context of the wisdom of Wu-wei if this Ignatian principle is to effect its aim.

One of the most vivid stories that I have come across that illustrates quite effectively Wu-wei is a scene from *Zorba the Greek*:

> I remembered one morning when I discovered a cocoon in the bark of a tree, just as the butterfly was making a hole in its case and preparing to come out. I waited a while, but it was too long in appearing and I was impatient. I bent over and breathed on it to warm it. I warmed it as quickly as I could and the miracle began to happen before my eyes, faster than life. The case opened, the butterfly started slowly crawling out and I shall never forget my horror when I saw how its wings were folded back and crumpled. The wretched butterfly tried with its whole trembling body to unfold them. Bending over, I tried to help it with my breath. In vain. It needed to be hatched out patiently and the unfolding of the wings should be a gradual process in the sun. Now it was too late. My breath had forced the butterfly to appear, all crumpled before its time. It struggled desperately and, a few seconds later, died in the palm of my hand.
>
> That little body is, I do believe, the greatest weight I have on my conscience. For I realize today that it is a mortal sin to violate the great laws of nature. We should not hurry, we should not be impatient, but we should confidently obey the eternal rhythm.

I have recalled with joy the moving and fruitful relationships I have had with directees whose lives have sometimes been very strongly marked by Buddhism, Confucianism, or Taoism. I have also been reminded again how important it is that a director be aware of these cultural-religious influences in order to accompany Asian retreatants more effectively.

In this brief exposition, I have concentrated on the first week of the Exercises because I feel an understanding of the basic principles of Buddhism, Confucianism, and Taoism, as they are correlated with the Ignatian principles, will be an invaluable help for the following weeks of the Exercises.

The Spiritual Exercises of St. Ignatius resonates with Buddhist concern

for the search for meaning and liberation of the self from all finite condi-
tioned existence. The Confucian father-child teachings and the "heaven-
endowed nature" doctrine connect with Christian-Ignatian experience of
God as Father and Creator of the nature which is heaven-directed. The
Taoist concern for the sacredness of the harmony and unity of the natural
course of things correlates with the Ignatian *"agere contra"* and the understanding of sin as a violation of the natural order which is part of the
Christian tradition.

The Spirit of God is the Director. However, Jesus has said, "The Holy
Spirit will give witness to me . . . and you will be my witnesses" (John 15:26–
27) and so the human director is called to collaborate with the Holy Spirit.
The director, through prayer and study where necessary, must try to become
more sensitive not only to the few correlative aspects that I have commented on, but also to the broad, general influences of Eastern philosophies
and cultures on Asians and non-Asians alike.

NOTES

1. "If the one giving the Exercises observes that the exercitant is in desolation
and tempted, the director should not be severe or harsh, but gentle and kind, giving
courage and strength for the future, exposing the wiles of the enemy of human
nature, and helping the exercitant to dispose the self for the consolation to come"
(Annotation 7). "If the one giving the Exercises perceives that the exercitant,
because of desolations and the wiles of the enemy, or because of consolations, has
need, the director may explain the rules of the first and second weeks for the
discernment of different spirits (cf. #313–327 and 328–336). *The Spiritual Exercises
of St. Ignatius*, a new translation by Elisabeth Meier Tetlow (Lanham, Md.: University Press of America), p. 5.

REFERENCES

Chan, W. T., trans. (1969). *A Source Book in Chinese Philosophy*. Princeton, N.J.:
Princeton University Press.
DeVos, G. A. (1973). *Socialization for Achievement: Essays on the Cultural Psychology
of the Japanese*. Berkeley, Calif.: The University of California Press.
Doi, T. (1962). "Amae: A Key Concept for Understanding Japanese Personality."
In R. J. Smith and R. K. Beardsley, eds. *Japanese Culture*. Chicago: Aldine.
Hsu, F. L. K. (1968). "Chinese Kinship and Chinese Behavior." In T. Tsou and P.
Ho, eds. *China in Crisis*, vol. one, book 2. Chicago: Chicago University Press.
Main Currents of Korean Thought. (1983). Ed. Korean National Commission for
UNESCO. U.S.A.: Pace International Research Inc.
Munro, D. J. (1977). *The Concept of Man in Contemporary China*. Ann Arbor, Mich.:
The University of Michigan Press.
Quintos, Lily. (1977). *Buddhism in Dialogue*. Manila, Philippines: Cardinal Bea
Institute.
Watts, Alan. (1940). *The Meaning of Happiness*. New York: Harper and Row.
Weber, M. (1951). *The Religion of China — Confucianism and Taoism*. Trans. H. H.
Gerth. Illinois Free Press.

9

Spiritual Direction in Japan

JOAN CONRAD, SSND

My contact with Japan began when I taught in Los Angeles in the 1950s and met some of our returning missionaries from that country. One day I casually said something to the effect of "If you think I would be of any help to the mission in Japan ... " Five years later, in 1961, I arrived in Japan and began what has now been thirty years of ministry here. After about ten years in the school apostolate, I felt a deep interior call that led to my community assigning me to the spiritual development apostolate. While receiving my formation and training for this ministry in St. Louis, I reflected on my experience of the Japanese church. It was at that time still a very Roman Church. Japanese Catholicism had not, on the whole, become indigenous and inculturated. We were still largely sharing our faith as a matter of legal observance.

As I entered into deeper formation in prayer under Jesuit direction, I realized that contemplative prayer was part of our heritage as Catholics. My thoughts returned to Japan, where there is such a deep respect and love for nature. In the traditional houses the movable sliding doors invariably open to a beautiful natural scene. This fosters a reflective response to life. As one turns back to the room itself, one faces the *tokonoma*. This is a recessed area in a tatami room that displays some article of beauty. The proper response to this is to take time to view it and share some words of appreciation. Then there is the tea ceremony, and the way of flower arranging, and the martial arts. These all require a deep contemplative stance toward the art and take years to acquire. There are more examples of this type, but I cite these because they are at the heart of everyday living. However, sad to say, this is becoming less and less true.

I realized that the contemplative heritage of our Church would be something that Japanese Christianity could respond to and develop and inculturate. Hopefully, it would eventually help the Church to become deeply rooted in the culture. Now, after being in this apostolate of spiritual development in which spiritual direction (which I prefer to call "spiritual companioning") is at the center, I know I had something in that thought that came from a much greater source than my store of inspiration. At the same time, I did not envision the way this apostolate would actually develop.

The Catholic Church in Japan does not even represent one-half of one percent of the total population. However, the number of women in religious communities represents a very high percentage of the total number of Catholics. So the need for formation for women in the art of spiritual direction was the need I initially began to address. Of course, this need was recognized in the larger Church at that time and especially in the American Church, so I had good backing and support from the Jesuits, who helped with my initial formation in setting up a program of ongoing formation here.

In 1975 we held our first thirty-day retreat for novice mistresses, provincials, and formation personnel. The response was so positive, and continues to be so, that there was never any doubt that there was a real need and an unconscious desire for this type of formation. At the present time we move all over the country, using existing retreat houses and their facilities, since the center that I am based in is quite small.

From the beginning we also offered this formation to priests who were interested in this apostolate. There is no possibility or desire to function without priests in this ministry, but the priests also had to desire to provide this formation for women. At first we began to use our developing skills on teams through offering private prayer direction on a weekend. These were open to laypeople, religious, and priests, with each weekend drawing a smattering of laity, but the majority was always religious women.

Among the priests who continued to attend our formation program was a Maryknoller, Tony Brodniak, who has shared the fulltime responsibility for this program with me for the past ten years. He was on several of our early teams, and he asked us to bring a team to the parish of which he was pastor for a long weekend retreat of private direction for people who were interested. This initial thrust into the parish community was the beginning of a part of our ministry that we value highly. We now go to parishes throughout the year when the pastor of the parish, at the request of his parishioners, invites us.

After the initial start with weekend retreats, we moved into offering privately directed eight-day retreats in all the vacation seasons. For years we continued to invite Jesuits, whose training and skills we appreciated, to supervise our direction in team meetings held daily on the spot and to give workshops to deepen our skills.

In the meantime, one of our Jesuit friends working here in a similar apostolate, who sometimes cooperated with us in our total program, went to the Institute for Spiritual Leadership in Chicago. This led to some fruitful contact between ourselves and the Institute. As a result, Tony and I were invited to attend the Institute. Tony participated in the progam in 1982, and I did so in 1983. As a result of that formation, we began to offer a seven-day workshop in self-discovery with Sister Sanae Masuda, RSCJ, also a graduate of the institute.

In this workshop Tony uses his knowledge and experience of the spiritual journey as described by Teresa of Avila, John of the Cross, Meister Eckhart, Ignatius Loyola, and so forth, and places it within a Jungian framework. This approach is based on Jung's description of the process of inner growth and development throughout life that occurs through deepening awareness of ourselves. Using Japanese myth and folklore, Sanae then presents the universal symbols found in every culture's myths and folklore. As members of the human race, we share a level of human responses that are common to all humanity and transcend culture and race. These Jung acknowledged by calling them archetypes. Sanae's work is to facilitate recognition of one's personal responses in dealing with these symbols. In my exercises, in order to foster a contemplative attitude toward oneself, I use the Jungian-based psychosynthesis exercises, as presented by Italian psychiatrist Piero Ferrucci, to facilitate the inner integration to which we are called in the second half of life.

To the people who attended this first workshop and who grew to the extent that they were hungering for more, we extended an invitation to a thirty-day institute. We offered our first thirty-day program in 1988. That year two priests, one laywoman, and nine sisters participated. In 1989 there were three laywomen and nine sisters, and in 1990, one priest, one laywoman, and nine sisters. We limit the institute to twelve persons for more effective group dynamics. The institute is held in a retreat house in a central location in the country.

The first week of this institute is devoted to further self-discovery. Tony's material is based on John of the Cross's outline of the "Dark Night of the Senses." He expands this with explanation of the same material by other mystics, such as Teresa of Avila and Eckhart. The terminology is both scriptural and Jungian. I continue with further psychosynthesis exercises, and Sanae does the same with Japanese folklore and myths. We both use our exercises to promote contemplative prayer and to deepen an ongoing awareness of self, which is one way to honor our call to "pray always."

After a day of rest, we move into Enneagram material, with Tony giving the theory and Sanae and I working with exercises that promote self-discovery in Enneagram terminology. After this week on the Enneagram and a day of relaxation, we go into a third week designed to facilitate further self-discovery. During this week, the three of us take equal time during lectures of an hour's length.

There are six topics that we consider fundamental to an understanding of our style of companioning people. The first is listening, and we present formation designed to further develop and deepen the listening ability of the participants. We feel that there is hardly an apostolate that would not benefit from a deeply developed ability to listen. This way of listening is designed to further growth in the person who is being companioned. This is followed by companioning, challenging, mutuality, the spiritual journey, and spirituality.

Each day, in order to integrate this theory into the person's own way of listening, the participants are involved in quadrads in which they successively take the role of traveler, or the one who is the companion, or one of the two observers in each group. One of the reasons we limit the group of participants to twelve is so that each of the three of us can be in one of the reflection groups. This reflection takes place after the interview between the companion and the traveler. All four members of the quadrad share their personal evaluation of the dynamic that has just taken place. Lastly, the team member presents his or her feedback. Thus we may be training someone to help on one of our teams promoting the privately directed eight-day retreat. Or this training may become helpful to the participants already involved in service to people in formation of one type or the other. It may also become helpful to those involved in a pastoral apostolate to the sick and in counseling situations. Finally, after another day of rest, we move into a final eight-day privately directed retreat, during which each one of us accompanies four of the participants in deepening the self-discovery gained in the first three weeks.

I have gone into much detail on the process that we use to promote contemplative prayer because the three of us have all had experience with other thirty-day retreat experiences and none has been nearly so effective. This may be due to the fact that we only accept people into the initial workshop and the thirty-day institute whom we have discovered to be able to pray contemplatively, that is, to pray with the heart. Such prayer usually produces profound change on many levels. Recognition of this interior change often takes place during an eight-day retreat companioned by one of us. We have decided to allow only people who are somewhat prepared and give promise of being able to pray contemplatively to participate, not because we want to foster elitism, but in order to ensure that the person is able to descend from the head to the heart; an experience that is at the heart of this kind of prayer formation. Without it, both traveler and companion will experience much pain.

I described this process in detail because it leads me to the central point I want to make. We have discovered that when people pray contemplatively, they begin to meet within themselves responses that are both individual and universal. Individual responses emerge from the person's personality and history. The response may come from the person as she or he has been formed by Japanese cultural, societal, and educational values. If so, that response would conform rather clearly to the norms of these value systems that are so strong in this group-oriented culture. At this level, one would be aware that the response has a distinctly Japanese flavor of perhaps "not rocking the boat," or "doing the pleasing thing," or "keeping all the rough edges underneath."

Universal responses become clear when people pray from the deep unconscious level of their being, where we are not limited by national or cultural boundaries. We cross over all barriers into an area that everyone shares because of our common humanity. Here we deal with desires and hopes that all people share, with responses toward pain and suffering, with childhood experiences with parents. In this last area we meet what happens to every child, no matter how good their parents were.

We find that the child needs to endlessly suppress his or her own natural and legitimate inclinations and adapt to the will of one or both parents. In doing this the child rejects certain aspects of its own God-given personality, which leaves wounds that deform or twist the child's response to life. These wounds usually remain hidden and rise up for integration and healing only when a person starts to pray contemplatively. When the person begins to take a contemplative attitude toward life, all that Providence has allowed to happen to that person that has been negative or destructive will begin to be presented to the person by her or his inner director so that it can be healed and accepted and gradually integrated into the person made in the image and likeness of the Creator. This Creator, who is also the ongoing author of that person in his or her development, is available to people who will risk descending from the sureness and safety of their heads to the mysterious and unpredictable regions of the heart. At the same time, if a person has the courage to travel this often difficult road, she or he begins to meet an inner strength that they are somehow able to recognize as belonging to an existence that is far superior to one's own and yet at the same time is part, in some mysterious way, of one's own totality.

This experience of God or the Divine gradually develops in the person the courage to go farther on the journey inward. And with each new encounter with what is painful or undeveloped, the courage grows to stay there in the contemplative posture, to dialogue with that inner Presence, or just to be there accepting the pain and suffering in the presence of that greater Presence. Finally this greater Presence brings the person through to a new area of health and growth and integration.

Another area of universal human experience is that of our emotions, sensations, images, and dreams. These are all very much part of the "heart" level of the inner journey. The content of the dreams and images may have cultural overtones affected by one's history within that culture, but there are many common images, especially in our dreams, which bond us as members of one human family.

Finally I must speak of what happens to me as I companion a person in prayer in a workshop devoted to deepening inner conversion and inner growth. First, as a team, we have gradually grown aware that as we continue our own journey, specifically as we live in deep awareness of ourselves at this moment of life, we are increasingly able to be helpful in enabling this process on an ever deeper level. But an even greater gift is given as I companion someone who begins to pray contemplatively. As he or she gets in touch with the deep responses that are common to us all as human beings, we both lose for the time being that which separates us as Japanese and American. I participate in the satisfaction that comes from understanding through my own experience that what the person is sharing is, on some level, experienced by everyone who is in the process of their own journey.

This universal process which is common to all people is available to people who pray contemplatively. But when this level is reached, I also feel understood, because my own experience is of a similar nature. I lose, temporarily, my foreignness in another country. Of course, after this is over, I go back to being a foreigner in Japan. But on some level I am changed through this experience. I am less a foreigner in Japan and more a member of the family of the earth.

Lastly, I need to say that when I first came to this culture, I thought I had to teach people here about God, and to some extent that is true. But at the same time, the Japanese have a culturally ingrained contemplative bent that prepares them, to an enviable degree, for contemplative prayer. They have an innate sense of the spiritual in nature and feel healed and refreshed from an encounter with nature. For example, their appreciation of one flower arranged just so in a vase and placed with studied care in the corner of the room, or an arrangement of bent and broken twigs with one or two flowers; their ability to take nature as it is and highlight one small aspect to make an aesthetic impression, all clearly show this. They value and respect what comes to them through their eyes when they rest on something that is beautiful or natural and what also comes to them through their ears when they allow themselves to reverberate with sounds in music and nature.

Rooted in this experience, what the physicists are saying about their discoveries about the nature of matter and what Eckhart and the other mystics said centuries ago in metaphorical terminology seem to me to be of the same essence. The abstract dimension and the indefinable in the contemplative nature of the Japanese have helped me sense God where I did not sense the divine Presence before.

Culturally, these people are heart people, but while they do not show this to the uneducated observer, discovering that they feel and respond deeply has been one of the great rewards of this work. It is this ability to respond on an affective level that has facilitated their entering into contemplative prayer and consequently the process of conversion leading to deeper growth and freedom. And it is in being a part of this that I have been taught, that I have been enriched, that I have been called to further growth.

As I have been enriched by my contact with the Japanese people in this culture, I have been enabled through my personal journey within this culture to become more fully a member of the universal human family which comes from only one source and that, of course, is God. I like to think that this experience of belonging to the human family has something to do with the Kingdom of God of which Jesus spoke so much and so familiarly. As Paul said: "There is no distinction between Jew and Greek; the same Lord is Lord of all and bestows his riches upon all who call upon Him" (Rom. 10:12). It is this vital unity that I experience so many times in my ministry. It has, indeed, been a deep and satisfying experience to live and work among my Japanese sisters and brothers.

10

Spiritual Direction and Religious Experience in the Cultural Environment of Brazil

PADRAIC LEONARD, CSSp

One hundred fifty years ago the cofounder of my congregation, Francis Libermann, wrote to a spiritual director: "Do not impose too many rules, do not follow a system in the spiritual life. Let grace act with great freedom." To a directee he wrote: "Regarding your mental prayer, follow your attraction and do not worry about the method."

Unfortunately, Libermann's advice was soon forgotten or ignored, and so during our formation we all said the same vocal prayers and were taught to meditate in the same way. Only after many years of routine prayer or no prayer are we becoming free to follow our attraction and so "let grace act with great freedom." This costly experience and a rediscovery of Libermann have convinced me of the importance of a great respect for the different ways in which people pray and relate to God.

My experience as an associate of the Center for Religious Development in Cambridge, Massachusetts, (1986–87) convinced me of the importance of not being overinfluenced by my own moral and dogmatic convictions in the exercise of this ministry. Clients of the center included "lapsed" Catholics, practicing homosexuals of both sexes, people involved in unions considered illicit or "sinful" by the church, drug users, zealous charismatics, women preparing for priestly ordination, priests, and religious. The only precondition was a sincere desire to find or improve their relationship to God and acceptance of weekly spiritual direction.

The culture-religious environment mix was mid-80s white American middle class, definitely a long way from the Irish Catholic culture I had grown up and been formed in (1925–50) and the liberation theology spirituality of my previous twenty years in Brazil.

But it was only after my return to Brazil in the fall of 1987 that I really began to take note of the difference that culture can make in religious experience and one's relationship with God. During a course I was directing, a young Bolivian brother volunteered to be directed. He had never moved outside his Indian village until at the age of nineteen he decided to become a religious. Now at twenty-nine he complained of having great difficulty in praying the way he had been taught by his formators. When I asked him about his image of Jesus, he revealed that his deepest experience of God's presence was in front of the Blessed Sacrament exposed during Benediction or Holy Hour. There he found himself praying as he had prayed as a child. On further inquiry I discovered that his tribe, now Catholic, had been what we would call "sun worshipers." The host in the monstrance, with its golden rays, was the nearest Catholic worship could come to this archetype.

A young Filipino religious on a directed retreat had prayed with a Gospel text and mounted on it for himself a series of rigid "musts" and "oughts" that he related to me in a sad and serious tone. When I wondered out loud what had happened to his native joy and optimism, he admitted that it had disappeared during his years of formation and community living with German formators and colleagues. When he recovered his original way of praying, his relationship with Jesus changed and the joy of life returned.

Brazil is a mixture of many cultures—interwoven, superimposed, distinct, clashing. Until 1500 C.E., Indians covered the geographic space that has since become Brazil. They have been exterminated or pushed into reserves in the south and center, forced into slavery in the northeast, cling precariously to life and native ways in the Amazon forests, and are barely touched by Christianity, which hasn't been able to attract them without corrupting their culture and castrating their customs.

The Portuguese colonists introduced their form of European culture. It included a religion based on practice rather than on morality: sacramental rites performed by priests and devotional rites performed by the laity. In a machismo, slavery-oriented society, there was little or no integration between the two.

When the supply of Indians ran out, slaves were imported from Africa. These were usually baptized on board ship or as soon as they reached land, in order to "guarantee their salvation." But whenever and wherever they could do so, they continued to practice their native cults secretly and transmit their beliefs to their children and the breast-fed children of their masters. At one time slaves outnumbered colonists by five to one, and today Rio de Janeiro is 70 percent colored and Salvador (Bahia) almost 90 percent.

Naturally there are cultural and religious differences between descendants of Yorubas, Ibos, and other African tribes, and these differences are reflected in the different spiritist cults practiced today: candomblé, umbanda, and their corruptions—kimbanda, macumba, saravá.

At the end of the last and beginning of this century, Brazil opened up to waves of immigrants from Germany, Italy, and Poland and later from Japan and Korea. So in Brazil one does not so much adapt to a "Brazilian" culture as try to be adaptable to a multitude of different cultures.

Besides the ethnic differences, there are the cultural and religious differences between a superaffluent 10 percent, a precarious middle class (20 percent), and the rest who form the "culture of poverty" or of misery, living below the recognized subsistence level.

Most vocations to religious and clerical life in Brazil are now coming from this "submerged" class. Many candidates are from broken or one-parent homes. They have known hunger, the promiscuity of overcrowded living, sexual abuse by father, stepfather, older brothers. These traumas must be worked through before they can have a healthy relationship with themselves, others, particularly those of the opposite sex, God the Father/Mother, Jesus. On the other hand, most formators and spiritual directors are still from the middle class, often European or trained in a European culture, who easily fail to recognize the deep spiritual values of this "culture of poverty." For example, with our individuality and rules of good conduct, we may miss the importance of *sharing* for them. They enjoy eating together from the same dish or plate (often using fingers only), sleeping in the same room, bathing together naked in the same pool or stream, and so forth.

Many are still being taught to pray "as the holy founder prayed." I have met several colored sisters who confessed that they could not pray. When asked to describe how they prayed as children or adolescents, their faces would light up as they described how they (and their parents) related to God or retold the religious experience that had led them to choose religious life in the first place. Some worried about their facility in going into alpha or even deeper states during prayer. They (or their formators) are inclined to identify this with the "trance" of the spiritist religions. Others have the sensitive's facility to pick up negative energy in another person or group as actual physical pain, and don't know what to do about it.

One result of being a member of an oppressed class or descendant of generations of slaves is an ingrained inferiority complex. This makes confrontation (especially by a foreigner) particularly difficult and delicate. Yet we know that confrontation is an essential part of any genuine helping relationship. Anything that smacks of criticism is classified as *feio* (ugly, nasty). It is even more *feio* when it happens in front of others. This makes group spiritual direction and supervision particularly difficult.

In addition, centuries of slavery had made suppression of anger a spontaneous reaction. The public expression of anger is always *feio*, and even to feel anger is regarded as sinful. Religious formation has tended to reinforce these convictions. Thus for anybody to admit anger against God takes a major effort. To express that anger directly to God is almost unthinkable. One wonders how much even God is allowed to be confrontative in such a culture.

A further result is that in this cultural context a spiritual director with a tendency toward authoritarianism or paternalism is sure to attract a number of dependent directees.

For in-depth spiritual direction it is important to help directees discover the images they have of God, not only those expressed under normal circumstances, but even more the unconscious ones that reappear in moments of crisis. Probably the most common popular image of God in Brazil is "one who chastises" even the innocent. All suffering is then "the will of God" and is unavoidable. Thus in the face of disaster and tragic loss the usual advice is "one must be resigned — it is the will of God."

Added to this sense of resignation is a firmly held belief in God as "the good Father" who takes care of all our needs, pardons all our sins, overlooks all our shortcomings. The contradiction between the two images is not adverted to. Both images combine in a kind of fatalism expressed in popular sayings such as: "God will provide," "nothing is going to change," and so forth. It is easy to find justification for belief in both in the Old Testament, especially the Psalms.

These images of God fit in well with the attitude of the dominant class and for centuries had the support of a Church intent on maintaining the status quo. Nowadays people seeking spiritual direction seldom speak of their experience of God in these images (except perhaps popular vocations in their early years). But in moments of crisis many revert to one or the other image, with resultant anger against God who "chastises" and/or the innocent or infantile dependence on the God who "provides."

It is not easy to discover the images people have of God. Even well-educated people may fear disbelief or shock if they reveal their most intimate image of God. I was giving a five-night retreat to members of a prayer group. While they prayed individually and shared in small groups, I walked back and forth in the brilliant moonlight of a tropical night. The thought struck me, "How pleased Jesus must be to be here tonight." Then I thought, "How pleased Jesus must be with me, for making all this possible." Feeling elated, I introduced a "skip-and-jump" into my walking.

I related this experience, with a demonstration, at the sharing session which followed. A fifty-year-old colored day laborer commented: "Funny, my Jesus always dances — but I would never have the courage to say so, had you not told me your experience." Come to think of it, what is more natural for an African or someone of African descent than a dancing Jesus? Can we as spiritual directors and formators win the confidence of a long-enslaved and oppressed people to the extent that they will reveal to us their non-European ways of relating to God? Even in Africa, I wonder how many will admit to a foreigner their belief in a dancing God?

Ways of experiencing and relating to God vary greatly between an individual-oriented and a communitarian culture. Brazilian middle-class (minority) spirituality is probably much the same as the North American and European type. Some people pursue religious experience as a "good" to be enjoyed or used as another "consumer product," producing personal satisfaction, protection, family welfare, consolation, guarantee of an eternity of heavenly affluence when we have to say "good-bye" to the earthly variety. Evangelization (when mentioned) means individual conversion (preferably via the mass media); expressions such as "preferential option for the poor," capitalist exploitation, liberation theology, and the overthrow of unjust structures are very threatening and uncomfortable.

In this private religious context, oblivious to the injustices of one's society, spiritual direction becomes a time to talk about a "comfortable" relationship with an undemanding God, with someone to listen sympathetically to your woes and psychological hangups who affirms pleasant experiences in prayer and suggests soothing Scripture texts.

Church community (where mentioned) is an hour a week in a carpeted church with an expensive sound system and laid-on services from salaried ministers, now mostly lay. Prayer groups concentrate on a relaxed, warm atmosphere, with prayers of intercession, healing services, and such. There often is a generous outreach to some underprivileged group, but no real commitment to challenge the reason why others are underprivileged in the first place.

While this sketch of middle- and upper-class spirituality might seem a bit overdrawn, it does express the truth spoken at Puebla in 1976 of "Rich people (and nations) becoming richer at the expense of poor people (and nations) becoming poorer."

The spirituality of the Brazilian poor in basic ecclesial communities is very different. God is still consoling and protective, but also very confrontative. He[1] challenges, defies, calls forth so that all may have life and not just a few. The Bible is proclaimed, prayed, and sung as commentary on everyday life, while the experiences of everyday life are told, prayed, and sung as commentary on the Bible.

It is very much an exodus spirituality. God is the one who "hears the cry of the poor and comes down" to invite the masses to become a people — his people. He promised to set that people free, and on the strength of that promise, the people struggle and undertake the long journey toward the promised land, passing through the purifying desert of suffering and sacrifice. There is a sense of a people making its history rather than having it made for them by the great and powerful. There are prophets, too, members of a prophetic church, and there are martyrs.

There is a tremendously strong spirit of sharing that is part of a deeply rooted cultural tradition. Speaking of tradition, the religious traditions of the people expressed through pilgrimage, patronal feasts, rites of passage, and pious customs are respected and celebrated, purified of the accretions of centuries. In these communities true friendships can exist. Men and women are equal, and indeed most elected ministers and leaders are women.

It is interesting to see the extent to which these basic ecclesial communities have the characteristics of group spiritual direction. Welcome is warm, sincere, and personalized. Listening is keen as people tell their story, especially the story of their experience of God. Everyone is listened to and meets with some response. There is empathy and respect for cultural differences and social stratification, with "the poor helping the poor." Subjects discussed are very real and deal with the "here and now." The linking of the Scriptures with life guarantees that God's action is contemplated in joy and sorrow, success and failure, struggle and leisure, strength and weakness. There is confrontation, since people often say one thing and do another. Leaders, ministers, and catechists take training courses and discover new images of God, of themselves, of the world and new terms of reference for community building. Discernment is needed as alternative lines of action are discussed. Action is decided on and assumed by all. There are moments of evaluation, celebration, and mutual encouragement as the community continues to grow and the Kingdom to come.

Newly arrived pastoral agents who work with these communities soon discover (if they are open enough) that they are moving away from an intellectual (head) approach to God and into an experiential (heart) area, the true area of relationship and spiritual direction. These agents then seek spiritual direction as a means of growth in the love of God and of the poor, as they try to discern not the easy way but "the good and perfect way."

In the struggle against unjust structures, failure is very evident and frequent. There is the temptation to divide the world into "friends" and "enemies," to despair, to violence. Prayer and spiritual direction are constantly needed if one is to continue to believe in an apparently impotent God, realizing that God's grace works more through human weakness than through strength. The words of the Psalmist come alive in the hearts of the people: "Their trust is in horses and chariots but ours in the name of the Lord" (Psalm 20:8).

Gustavo Gutiérrez speaks of this creative moment in Latin America as a new spirituality is born from their own experience of poverty and oppression:

> The struggles of the poor for liberation represent an assertion of their right to life. The poverty that the poor suffer means death: a premature and unjust death. It is on the basis of this affirmation of life that the poor of Latin America are trying to live their faith, recognize the love of God, and proclaim their hope. Within these struggles, with their many forms and phases, an oppressed and believing people is increasingly creating a way of Christian life, a spirituality.[2]

The poor are becoming the subject of their own spirituality, no longer an object, as in the past.

Just as members of the affluent society are tempted by an overly *ad intra* spirituality, those who fight for a just society are often tempted by an overly "incarnated" or *ad extra* spirituality, leading to activism and burnout. Both forms need confrontation, but the second, being more communitarian and open to challenge, is more liable to accept confrontation. Unfortunately there is often mutual recrimination, one "camp" accusing the other of being "all prayer and no action" or "all action and no prayer," not realizing that there exists a middle way. Both groups and types of individuals need to be listened to in spiritual direction and helped along the road to integration.

In Brazil, older religious tend in general toward an individualistic piety, even while living in large "communities," while younger ones tend to be more communitarian, even when living in communities of two or three. Those who were born poor but "formed" into middle-class values have greater difficulty in moving back toward the poor than those who were born rich or middle class.

A study of the archetypes of the various cultures in Brazil would be very helpful for spiritual directors, but such a study has not yet been undertaken. We have mentioned the "Sun God" of the Bolivian brother and the "dancing God" of the Africans. A Nissei (born in Brazil to Japanese parents) colleague is about to publish a doctoral thesis[3] that he defended at the University of Fribourg (Switzerland) after spending a year at the Jungian Institute of Zurich. In it he traces the links in Brazilian culture between Yemenjá, Yoruba female deity of the sea, and Our Lady. The forbidden African cult was practiced during the centuries of slavery under the syncretic guise of devotion to Mary Immaculate. How much Yemenjá and how much Mary is the female archetype of present-day Catholic cult would be hard to tell. Similarly the Indians have Mother Earth, *La Pacha Mama*, as a strong archetype, and she is often identified with Mother Mary.

A barrier to growth in both human and divine relationships in Brazil is the absence of a cultural archetype for man–woman friendship. Men see women as either wife/mother or mistress. (A prostitute isn't even a woman; she is a *puta*, a despised sexual object.) Women see men as either husband/ father or lover. A side-effect of this in spiritual direction is a certain predisposition to transference and/or countertransference on the affective level. If every friend of the opposite sex is unconsciously seen as future partner or lover, the "soul friend" can easily be cast in one of these roles.

An additional risk in this connection is the Brazilian "abraço." It is normal courtesy to embrace and touch cheek to cheek on meeting and on parting. One of the first signs of transference and/or countertransference is when the parting embrace becomes prolonged or more intense than usual. The director must be very alert to signs of transference in the directee and countertransference within herself or himself.

A culturally weak father image and a strong mother image lead to greater reliance on Mary as Mother than on God as Father. Popular devotion to Jesus is almost unknown. He is confused with the Father, or for many he is simply another powerful saint: "São Salvador." The pure and immaculate

Mary is a model for wives and daughters, but Jesus is never seen as a model for husbands and sons.

Archetypes become even more important if we decide to work with dreams in spiritual direction. During a directed retreat an Irish colleague had a series of revealing dreams about boats. Not only was his family very interested in boats, but his name in translation means Son of the Hound of the Sea.

There is a delicate balance between helping a directee go deeper into his or her experience and respect for the inviolable intimacy of that experience. Most directees find this accompanied exploration helpful in discovering new aspects of their experience. However, a woman pointed out to me that men are naturally more prone to probe, while women are more likely to accept passively what is recounted to them. Women may resist what they unconsciously or consciously consider an intrusion into their privacy or may later feel that they have been in some way violated or led into revealing more than they would have wished. A sign of this may be a feeling of shame at meeting their director in everyday life. In the past, of course, the confessional was a tremendous source of abuse in this respect.

In a macho society such as Brazil, the tendency to prefer a priest as spiritual director is not entirely due to tradition and clericalism. Most men (and especially priests) have difficulty in accepting a woman as spiritual or retreat director, and many bishops will not permit sisters as spiritual directors for their seminarians.

Finally, a new feature of the religious environment in Brazil is the interest in an integrated or holistic approach to health. This may have begun as a pragmatic response to the fact that the vast majority of the population cannot afford traditional medical care or pharmaceutical medicines and do not have access to the bureaucracy-riddled national health service. The people have their own herbal and natural cures and diets that are being widely recovered and encouraged, especially by pastoral agents. Among the upper classes, the holistic approach of the northern hemisphere is also exerting a certain influence. Several centers offer mud, air, sun, water treatment as well as massage, naturally produced diets, herbal treatment, and so forth. They also offer training courses for pastoral agents working in the health field.

There are some signs that this holistic approach is beginning to influence the field of spiritual direction, such as body massage during directed retreats, use of yoga, interaction and collaboration between spiritual directors, psychologists, and natural-health specialists. All this is in its infancy. The trichotomy of body, soul, and spirit (emotions) is still very evident as each receives separate "treatment." A center or series of centers that would deal at the same time with all three and train pastoral agents to work with the poor on all dimensions at once is still a dream, but a dream that will hopefully one day come true.

From my limited experience, I would conclude that spiritual direction based on the contemplative approach will discover the divine in any culture. To be a good spiritual director involves a listening that is sensitive to the different at all levels: culture, language, religious beliefs, values, social context, and so forth. It involves an openness to the new and the surprising. It means walking along with rather than judging, directing, advising. After all, the important relationship is that between directee and God. After God is the directee, not the director, whose role is limited and secondary. I believe that a spiritual direction based on these criteria is adaptable to any situation or culture.

NOTES

1. Inclusive language has not yet become a feature of Brazilian spirituality.
2. Gustavo Gutiérrez, *We Drink from Our Own Wells*, trans. Matthew J. O'Connell (Maryknoll, N. Y.: Orbis Books, 1984), p. 28.
3. Pedro Kuniharu Iwashita, CSSp, *Maria no Contexto da Religiosidade Popular Brasileiro.*

11

Spiritual Direction in Chile: Confronting the Experience of Oppression

ANN BELLIVEAU, SSA

It is impossible to mention all the facets of spiritual direction as lived and practiced in South America, and specifically in Chile. Therefore, my focus will be on how spiritual direction has been one of the vehicles used to help free persons who have lived under a military government and have been psychologically wounded by its unjust practices from 1973 to March 1990. There is not a strata of Chilean society that was not marked by this controlling system with its constant violation of human rights.

To a great extent, the Catholic Church became the voice of the voiceless. The people of God were supported spiritually, psychologically, and socially by the members of this caring community. In solidarity, it became a common practice to reflect prayerfully on their lack of freedom. It was in those Christ-centered groups reflecting on the themes of liberation and freedom and seeking practical solutions to their situations of oppression that gave birth to Liberation Theology. Bereft of hope in the governing body of the state, they turned to their God who liberates and constantly calls them to an alliance of fidelity. This is a call to the faith that does justice, but more often than not, those active in work for justice are without the support of the faith.[1]

In their distress, the Chileans turned to the Church and its ministers: pastor, religious, or lay leader, asking for all types of assistance. This initial contact was not to seek spiritual help, but rather physical, psychological, and material aid.

The religious workers are actively engaged in defending the rights of the people. Some specific forms of acting were encouraging and accompanying a person to Solidaridad (an organization of the Santiago diocese dedicated to defending human rights[2]) to denounce his or her specific experience of injustice, going from one police station to another in search of a *disaparecido* (a missing person, assumed taken prisoner by the military for political reasons), and being supportive in other types of experiences.

These contacts of the Chilean people with church ministers marked the beginning of a healthy relationship. The Gospel-inspired actions of church members attracted many persons and groups, and they began to frequent church activities. They often became involved in religious formation through a prayer group, a Bible reflection group, a *Comunidad Ecclesial de Base* (ecclesial-based communities), or pastoral movements for the workers. This is only to mention a few types of Christian formation groups. More importantly, many persons who were whole-heartedly dedicated to Gospel values were trained and given leadership roles in the church, either in the main church or a branch chapel.

After this lengthy process of formation, it was noticed that persons moved from justice issues to faith issues, from action to prayer, and from social commitments to spiritual commitments. One of the most important fruits of this formation was the realization conveyed to each person of her or his worth as a person and that each person is especially loved by God and worthy of respect and dignity. Persons engulfed in this social, cultural, political, and religious change need continually to reflect on and question their lives and experiences. Questions such as these are most crucial:

How can anyone be led to an authentic encounter with Jesus, Lord of History, in his mission?

How and where do we meet the historical Jesus who builds his Reign today in our world?[3]

It is crucial for us, as formators of Christian leaders, to be aware of the fact that some persons are pondering these questions and that they are in need of personal support and encouragement. Indeed, they are requesting it. They are approaching the historical Jesus in what may appear to be a paradoxical way. Some persons are active and enthusiastic in a movement dedicated to Jesus while wondering who he is and how his charism, magnetism, and goodness have attracted so many disciples to his mission. Thus is born the desire to know Jesus better.[4]

This step of desiring to know Jesus better is a noteworthy one in Chile for an important reason. Although the country is considered a Catholic nation, for the most part its members derive their sense of belonging to the Church through minimal participation. Their innate faith is more easily expressed in popular religious practices, rather than in the sacramental life of the Church.

This essay focuses on Chilean Christians who, after having spent many years in a routine faith relationship with the Lord, now desire to embark on a more intimate bond. This desire may spring from personal or cultural needs but is definitely motivated by the Spirit. These persons are the most likely to seek out spiritual direction in the context of a retreat or outside of it.

In summary, the Chilean who has been involved in the work of the Kingdom and has been wooed by the magnanimity of its leader, Jesus, is most likely to seek spiritual direction in order to know Christ more intimately and love him more profoundly. Of course, this is not the only reason why a person may desire spiritual direction. For example, religious often experience direction as a means of continuing formation in order to deepen their existing relationship with the Lord.

Having sketched in broad strokes something of the religious, cultural, and political background of Chilean Christians and their motivation in spiritual direction, I would now like to describe some of the specific cultural responses seen in the direction relationship. These responses differ in their emotional intensity from other cultures, although the basic movements are the same in all cultures. The order in which they will be enumerated is not necessarily that of importance.

One of the most basic skills that facilitates spiritual direction is the directees' ability to communicate their feelings and their story. This ability to share has been cultivated since infancy within the extended family environment. Chileans are very dynamic conversationalists. It is extremely important for the director to listen attentively to their story, their desires, their sufferings.[5] Many have deep, open wounds from painful family experiences, and there is often unvoiced anger and a feeling of unworthiness in the eyes of God.

Important to them is the awareness of certain movements in their prayer, and they wonder what the Lord is trying to tell them through such experiences. In fact, they are trying to discern the spirits. Often exaggerated emotional responses are elicited. These powerful emotions vibrantly express the sense of *el sentir* of which Ignatius of Loyola speaks, an experience of being dearly loved by their Creator and especially being called by name. They also enter deeply the darkness of sinfulness and awareness of sinful tendencies within themselves with strong feelings of contrition. (These are truly graced moments, since within the Chilean culture it is very difficult for a person to admit to wrongdoing or even a small infraction.)

The director may suggest that all of these movements be brought to prayer so that they can be reflected upon carefully and profoundly. It is very important to seek a firm foundation through the quality of the dialogue with the Lord and a persevering relationship. These two will form excellent criteria with which to judge the authenticity of the religious experience.

Because feelings are such a strong barometer in their lives, it is important that they reflect on their continuing journey under the guidance of a director in order to be able to live effectively through the moments of desolation as well as of consolation, knowing that in both states the Lord is always present. This helps their prayer to continue to be vibrant and relevant to their lives as they are encouraged to stand transparent before the Lord.[6]

The Chileans are truly in contact with their daily experiences and so it is crucial for them to reflect on past experiences, including the feeling of powerlessness that existed (and has not yet totally disappeared) in the social, economic, and psychological areas of their lives. This feeling of powerlessness, so akin to the first Beatitude of poverty of spirit of which St. Matthew speaks, forms the basic foundation upon which they build their spiritual lives. In the midst of all their insecurities, anxieties, and sufferings, they are a people of faith whose hope is always in the Lord.

Because of their weak foundation of doctrinal knowledge of the faith and their involvement in traditional, popular religious practices, it is often difficult for them to bring their religious experiences to a truly reflective awareness. It is difficult for Chileans to say who God is for them, especially if their image of God is of "father" and their relationships with their own fathers have been negative. It is to be underlined here that machismo is very strong in the Chilean culture. Fathers tend to be very dominating, while both parents are very possessive of their offspring.

Their past history in the family is often difficult to own; the wounds are deep and the hurts well recorded. Before these persons can perceive the trajectory of their relationship with God, they must know how God has led them to see realistically the course of their spiritual journey. The whole growth and development of a person's spiritual journey is indispensably linked to their image of God. Often they deal with what I term *el Dios de los negocios* — God the businessman. In faith they barter with him, but with little belief in the "gifts without string" that God bestows on them: "If you grant me this, Lord, I shall do such and such." Many times they promise to do a pilgrimage to a shrine (miles away, at a cost they can ill-afford), crawling toward the sanctuary on their knees. Or they may be semiparalyzed by the image they have of God who punishes any and all wrongdoings. A director can help people clarify their image of God within their personal history.

The important function of affirmation by the spiritual director is important in all cultures, but especially here in Chile it is crucial for women, where their selfless giving is expected and is taken for granted. It is in acknowledging her uniqueness as a free gift of the Lord that the woman becomes fully transformed by the Spirit and loses her poor self-image as she begins to believe that she is profoundly loved and cherished by the Lord.

Once she is convinced of her unique gifts to promote change in the world, she can play an important role in society and in the church. Some women have demonstrated this by assuming leadership roles in their chapels as teachers and formators of other lay leaders. More dramatically, some have organized demonstration groups, demanding to know the whereabouts of their *disaparecidos* (missing sons and/or husbands). Recently they have also confronted the judicial office to demand the release of the political prisoners of the last military government.

All of us living within the confines of a certain culture unconsciously assume the values of that culture. This is all the more noticeable if an unjust, irrational, repressive military system has been superimposed. Such an imposition on personal freedom readily promotes a very strong personal defensive reaction on the part of individuals who are likely to usurp other's rights or at least consider their own rights before those of their neighbors. Examples of actions such as consistently crossing the street on a red light are unconscious reactions to being unable to make decisions in their lives.

The director may suggest that the directees examine their value systems so that they can realize the dynamics in operation in their lives and readily confront their values with those of the Gospel. This will ensure that the directees will identify priorities for themselves in order to continue their spiritual journey authentically.[7]

Obsessed with the multiple demands of daily life in an oppressed society, Chileans find their lives scattered. Their concentrated efforts are to survive. To put aside this frenetic type of living even for a short time is difficult. It is hard for them to center themselves and find their innermost "still-point" in the Lord. The silent and quiet atmosphere of a retreat house is a radical change from the sound-polluted neighborhoods, the close quarters of their homes, and the continual social chatter so agreeable to their extended family living. To integrate all these elements is a tremendous challenge, especially for one new to the spiritual journey.

It is possible that some Chileans from the northern Atacama Desert region of the country would have literally lived in the desert. In the life of the Spirit, a desert experience is also probable, especially for those sincerely probing the more profound depths of their being. The apparent absence of the Lord leaves one feeling isolated in the dryness of desert life. All of one's personal efforts seem to yield no change in the feeling of abandonment. This painful experience of poverty is the Lord's grace that helps one realize that sanctity is initiated and nurtured through God's loving care, notwithstanding all our weaknesses, discouragement, and inertia. The spiritual director's role is a supportive one in these phases of the directees' spiritual journey so that they will not fall prey to discouragement and, by ceasing to make efforts to be connected with their innermost center, settle for a comfortable mediocrity.

Because of all of the "unfreedoms" in the Chileans' lives (especially from 1973 to March 1990), it is imperative to help the directees grasp some understanding of spiritual freedom and how it relates to fully living out their Christian faith. It is good for the director to listen and encourage whatever may surface on this theme. It is crucial for the directee to desire the experience of becoming spiritually free and to come to an awareness of some areas of her/his life where freedom is needed.

Given the countless experiences of injustices suffered, both personally and as a nation, it is very common to hear references to the persons who were instruments of these misdeeds. Negative feelings still abound against military personnel, the police, and the politicians supportive of the military regime. These past wounds are deep and painful; there are unconscious (and at times conscious) desires for revenge and vindication. These effects of sin influence present reactions and judgments and hold one captive.

If nothing emerges from the directee's prayer that touches this theme, and if there is no allusion to spiritual freedom, it may be wise for the director to introduce the theme of freedom, and above all, pardon. The following questions should be asked:

1. Is there an awareness of "unfreedoms" in their lives?
2. Is there a desire to become spiritually free?
3. Is there a willingness to expose past wounds in order to work toward healing?
4. Is there the desire to confront anxieties and other negative emotions that presently seem to paralyze their mode of living?

Freedom cannot be had without active involvement in these issues. It is important to relate to the directees' level of growth at this time and attempt to encourage them to continued openness to the action of the Spirit in their lives.

The above questions would form part of an ongoing discernment done within an atmosphere of prayer. The process of discernment is a simple but disciplined process. It is very important for Chileans, who are much more accustomed to making decisions on the spur of the moment according to their feelings, to have this experience of slow and profound discernment.

As the person approaches the decision to be made, important questions form the center of the process: "What do I feel God calling me to? Am I living my gifts while working for the Kingdom, the mission of the Church today?" During the process of discernment, the individuals need the accompaniment of the director, whose prayerful presence helps to affirm them. There is no limit to the sacrifices dedicated Chileans are willing to make for the sake of the Kingdom.

The sacred Scriptures are always an inspiration to Chilean Christians. They relate very well to certain books of the Old Testament, especially Genesis, Exodus, and the Psalms, which deal with themes of slavery and freedom, fidelity and infidelity: realities of Chilean life that make Yahweh very present to them and to their world today. God's ever-present fidelity to the chosen people is an awesome reality to them. They are touched very profoundly and find their hope for the present and the future.

Any creative renovation, any spirituality, has its sources in the Gospels. The historical Jesus has been "re-owned," and it is impossible to separate his living experience from the lives of the poor. The people are reflecting on the Gospels more frequently, especially through the C.E.B.s (ecclesial-based communities). These reflection groups have succeeded in helping numerous people correct their distorted image of the Christ of popular religiosity and embrace the God who walks with them today in their everyday reality.

These are some Scripture texts that relate to the life of Jesus that I have found significant in the life of some of the people I have directed:

The Freedom of Christ before the Political Powers (Matthew 22:15–21)
The Annunciation and Visitation (Luke 1:26–56)
Jesus Proclaims the Liberation of the Oppressed (Luke 4:16–21)
The Samaritan Woman (John 4:1–26) — How has Jesus broken into my life to give me what God is offering?
The Multiplication of Loaves (John 6:1–14)
The Woman Caught in Adultery (John 8:1–11)
Freedom in the Spirit (Galatians 5:1–25)
The Passion Narratives

Mary is very important to the people of Latin America as a model of those Christians dedicated to the poor and to evangelization. As servant of the Lord, Mary cooperated with God in a unique liberating action. Her fidelity in following Jesus in that precise historical time makes Mary a true model of Christian living.

Much has been written on the spirituality of Latin America today, and this material would be pertinent and very valuable to the subject of spiritual direction. Especially important to mention are the themes of suffering and death as contemplated in the life of Jesus, which have a tremendous impact on the Latin American. Their hope and faith are sharply focused on the Resurrection.

An entire people is marching forward to construct a world in which people are more important than material things, a world in which they may live in dignity and respect. A society respecting human liberty is placed at the service of the common good. This is what is seen as an historical process of liberation in all parts of the continent. The process is not advancing triumphally and is not without multiple obstacles, nor is it acclaimed by the entire world, nor has it reached every corner of the South American continent. But this is a small view of a process that is beginning to change the whole direction of the continent.

This essay has been written in order to share some experiences and observations in the ministry of spiritual direction in Chile. It is not a scientific study. The sampling of persons whom I have had the privilege of accompanying is far too limited in numbers and diversity of ages and cultures.

My own earthen vessel carries the richness of each one's story: the pain, the hopes, and the sufferings, as well as the impressive gifts of faith each

one has shared with me. Through these privileged hours with these directees, I have felt the Divine Potter fashioning me.

NOTES

1. Katherine Marie Dyckman, SNJM, and L. Patrick Carroll, SJ, *Inviting the Mystic, Supporting the Prophet* (New York: Paulist Press, 1981), p. 3.

2. This organization closed its office officially since the country's return to democracy.

3. Dyckman and Carroll, p. xi.

4. Ibid., p. xii.

5. Shaun McCarty, ST, "On Entering Spiritual Direction," *Review for Religious* 35 (1976), p. 859.

6. Ibid., p. 860.

7. Ibid.

12

Companion on Pilgrimage:
The Hispanic Experience

ADELE J. GONZALEZ

By acknowledging themselves to be strangers and foreigners on the earth, they showed that they were seeking a homeland . . . they were searching for a better, heavenly home.

Hebrews 11:13–16

Hispanics in the United States are a people on a journey. The sense of movement, of change, of alienation makes them a living reminder to all peoples that as Christians we are not yet fully "home."

The theme of the III Encuentro National Hispaño de Pastoral (Third National Hispanic Pastoral Encounter), Pueblo de Dios en Marcha (People of God on the Move), held in August 1985 in Washington, D.C., described the Hispanic presence in our midst. Hispanics are a young, dynamic force with a prophetic voice and a promise of vitality for the Church in the United States.

Hispanic peoples are extremely diverse. Southwest Hispanics whose roots in the United States go back for generations still find themselves feeling like aliens in their own country. Mexicans continue to move north, searching for better opportunities for their families; people from the islands have been migrating to the eastern seaboard, and the serious conditions in Central and South America continuously bring new migrations to our coasts. Some experts now estimate a total U.S. Hispanic population of at least 20 million people.

The United States today ranks fifth among the world's Spanish-speaking countries; only Mexico, Spain, Argentina, and Colombia have more Hispanics. They vary in color, history, racial origins, and sometimes in the ways

121

they express their faith. But despite differences, certain cultural similarities characterize them.

In their 1984 Pastoral Letter on Hispanic Ministry, "The Hispanic Presence: Challenge and Commitment," the U.S. bishops stated that among the values that make up the Hispanic culture are "a profound respect for the dignity of each person . . . a deep and reverential love for family life . . . a marvelous sense of community that celebrates life through fiesta . . . a loving appreciation for God's gift of life and an understanding of time which allows one to savor that gift . . . and an authentic and consistent devotion to Mary."

How do these cultural values affect the way Hispanics perceive God, life, and one another? Can the understanding of culture be of assistance to those in the ministry of spiritual direction? What is it like to be a female spiritual director within the Hispanic community? How do Hispanics understand spiritual direction?

As I reflect on my journey as a Hispanic woman in this ministry, I can see these questions surfacing over and over again. Hopefully this essay will offer some insights into the old familiar questions while raising new ones, even if at this moment in history we are not yet ready to deal with their answers.

We know that spiritual direction focuses on the directee's relationship with God as it is experienced in that person's life. Therefore, how people see God and life is a key element in the understanding of their response to God's activity in their everyday experiences.

As I have mentioned, one of the values of Hispanic culture is a deep and reverential love for family life. Among Hispanics, the person is never seen as an isolated unit, but as a member of a family system, a person in relationship with others. In this culture, you are a wife, a mother, a husband, or a father, a son, a sister, a cousin, a grandmother. You are an aunt or an uncle, and even an in-law. Often you wonder if there is anybody you know who is not related to you at all!

In the poor barrios, frequently children are raised by neighbors or godparents who assume that responsibility because of illness, financial difficulties, or absence in the nuclear family. In Hispanic families, parents and adults serve the children, and usually the elderly stay home and are cared for by their families for the rest of their lives. Parents expect and frequently receive respect from their children. In the very hierarchical Hispanic family system, parents make all the decisions and children obey. Often this becomes a very tyrannical situation. Hispanics are very warm and loving people and although love is expressed in many ways, parents are expected to demonstrate their love by providing for and disciplining their children.

Against this backdrop, it is easy to see God as Father, Jesus as *el hermano mayor* (the oldest heavenly brother), and Mary as *nuestra madre celestial* (our heavenly Mother). In my personal experience, I find many Hispanics who see God as the personal Father who provides for their every need, but who also disciplines them and is disappointed when they do not behave properly. Sometimes, if they feel a little intimidated by the father figure or experience him as busy and inaccessible, they do just what they usually do in their everyday life — they talk to their mother and ask her to talk to their father on their behalf. Thus, love and devotion to Mary is an integral part of Hispanic spirituality. She is their mother, the gentle woman who nurtures them. It is no wonder that every Hispanic culture honors Mary and that she has a very special place in the hearts of the people.

On the other hand, Jesus, the elder brother, is closer to their humanity. He is a companion in the journey, someone who walks with them in their joys and sorrows and who understands suffering and rejection. I know a teacher who insists, every time we meet, on having an empty chair with us as a living reminder of Jesus' very real presence when we are gathered in his name.

Many of the Hispanics to whom I minister love the Emmaus story found in Luke 24:13–35. They relate to the man who walks with them, listens to their story, and shares of himself in the breaking of the bread. They also find special meaning in the Passion narratives. My own experience teaches me that most Hispanics relate to the suffering Jesus to a degree that I usually do not find among my other directees. There is something about the intensity of the agony at Gethsemane, the loneliness of the Via Dolorosa, or the pain of Golgotha that touches the heart of Hispanic spirituality and their passionate way of loving.

My Hispanic directees appreciate comments or reflections on my part about Jesus' willingness to suffer for each one of us. There is a profound attraction for a God who shares our humanity and our pain. In fact, sometimes I find it very challenging to be able to share with them a God who wants us to be happy and who has come so that we may have life to the fullest (John 10:10).

In my ministry in the Archdiocese of Miami, as well as in other parts of the country, I encounter Hispanic people from different socioeconomic backgrounds. In spite of differences, they all seem to share this love for the cross. Such love may be triggered by their own poverty or by their fascination for Don Quixote figures, those people who are willing to fight windmills to achieve their impossible dreams. Personally, I have been challenged time and again to take a closer look at the physical pain and the emotional anguish of our crucified Lord. This love of the cross is seldom present among my other directees who are more influenced by the success-oriented values of the American culture.

Another important value in the Hispanic culture is their profound respect for the dignity of each person. For most Hispanics, people are above structures, systems, and programs. As a rule, their loyalties are more to people than to ideological systems. They more readily follow a person than a concept. Because of this, Hispanics may appear disrespectful or undisciplined. They are prone to protest against and oppose systems and structures that do not protect the individual. They may also ignore rules and laws when they become ends in themselves and stop serving the person's well-being.

I often find myself encouraging my directees, especially those in the south Florida area, to work within systems rather than to dismiss them as useless because of their impersonality. For the most part, Hispanics in the United States find it difficult to function within the American structures. Some groups embrace the values of the dominant culture and join the competitive and success-oriented American society. Others, because of poverty and lack of a solid education, withdraw and allow systems to oppress them and to dictate their lives. Thus spiritual directors in Hispanic communities need to have a clear understanding of this reality. We need to make sure that we do not support injustices and discrimination by guiding our directees to be submissive and passive.

Hispanics are usually a faith-filled people seeing everything as coming from God. Frequently, I find that this beautiful gift can be their worst enemy when it influences a fatalist outlook that interprets their problems and difficulties as God's will, thus rendering them powerless to bring about change or improve conditions. This attitude of total acceptance to life as it comes may offer a comfortable, pseudo-peace for the person, but it has also been used by systems and even people to keep Hispanics and other minority groups oppressed and discriminated against. Spiritual directors need to listen attentively to God's action in each person and help them discern when they are being called to a deeper trust and surrender and when they need to claim the dignity of the person that they so highly value.

For Christians, this cultural value proves helpful in terms of discipleship or the following of Jesus. Most Hispanics enjoy a personal relationship with the Lord and are trying very hard to follow him. A love for the Sacred Heart or for the crucified Lord permeates all of their lives.

The difficulty that I sometimes encounter with this attitude is that this experience of the love of Jesus does not always grow and develop parallel to a clear understanding of the Gospel message that challenges us to see him even in the least of our sisters or brothers (Matthew 25:31–46). At one end of the spectrum, I know people who remain caught in the "love of the Lord" experience while having difficulty engaging in ministry or social service. At the other end, I find those who see service as prayer, even at the risk of neglecting the quality of their personal time with the Lord in whose name they serve. In my experience, this is the key temptation of Hispanic ministers: the "doing" becomes the prayer, and not the other way around. My task is to invite them continually to establish a rhythm of prayer and ministry that enables them to grow in their relationship with a personal Lord while contributing to enhance the quality of the lives of their brothers and sisters.

When we mix this respect for the dignity of each person with their "marvelous sense of community that celebrates life through fiesta" that the U.S. bishops mentioned, we have an explosive combination. People are important; life is a gift; and Hispanics will find any excuse to celebrate both. Birthdays, baptisms, first communions, weddings, funerals, or a simple visit with friends is an opportunity for sharing meals, singing, or telling stories. Hispanics do not celebrate alone, and any event has the potential to become a fiesta.

I find Hispanics, as Catholics, more interested in celebrating their experience of God and community than in keeping their faith pure and free from error. My Hispanic directees are frequently open to popular expressions of their faith and tolerant of practices that are more rooted in their own personal experience of God than in the Church's teachings about God. This is one of the reasons why liturgical celebrations, especially the Eucharist, are so important in Hispanic spirituality. The worst thing that can happen to this festive people is for them to become trapped into a rigid, finely structured liturgy where they do not feel at home. Unless they have opportunities to celebrate God and life in a vibrant communal experience, they turn to more private devotions, such as the rosary, adoration of the Blessed Sacrament, novenas, and so forth. Because of their sense of journey as a pilgrim people, processions are also extremely important in the Hispanic religious expression.

When directees express dismay or frustration at the way they are practicing their faith, I believe it would be wise to look into how their cultural values are affirmed and celebrated in their parishes. Sometimes it is easier to blame it on their lack of piety and not take into consideration whether and how the community is calling forth their gifts and unique ways of expressing their faith.

According to the U.S. Census Bureau report of August 1987, 24.7 percent of Hispanics in the United States live below the poverty level. Society labels them migrants, minority groups, Hispanics, Latinos, Spanish-speaking. God calls them sons and daughters. I do believe that spiritual directors need to walk with these people and help them enter more fully into the awareness of this dignity. Their baptismal certificate could become the best I.D. card any Hispanic possesses and displays with pride.

Perhaps the cultural characteristic most frequently associated with Hispanics is their understanding of time, which allows them to savor God's gift of life. This attitude is often perceived as "Hispanics always being late" or "having no sense of time." The fact is that they never seem to be in any hurry to get anywhere. In my experience among different Hispanic peoples, time for them is now. They are oriented to the present and have a tremendous ability to enjoy every moment to the fullest.

In spiritual direction, it is important to remember this way of looking at time. Hispanics meet their God in the present and tend to become impatient with any process that is too future oriented. Thus prayer is very relational and emotional and frequently has a deep sense of urgency, since it is usually connected to the immediate reality of life and family. Because of this attitude, I have found the Book of Psalms a very helpful tool to enrich prayer life, especially in the early stages of spiritual growth.

Perhaps this is the area where all the cultural values that I have mentioned converge. In prayer, Hispanics celebrate the gift of life in all its manifestations. Joy and sorrow, pain and healing, petition and thanksgiving are all expressed when they encounter their Lord in prayer. Prayer is also a family experience. Family is holy ground and, for the most part, faith is transmitted in the home. Mary is an integral part of it, and the rosary is perhaps the most favored devotion among Hispanics. For spiritual directors, an understanding of how their directees see life and where they meet God is crucial if they want to assist them in deepening their prayer life. In this way we continue to see the relation of faith and culture in lived experience.

As a Hispanic woman myself, I have to make adjustments to meet my directees in their own cultural milieu. Among Hispanics, I find myself playing the role of spiritual mother more frequently than that of guide or companion. This is even more significant with male directees. With them my challenge is to affirm and call forth the feminine dimension of their personality and, in the midst of a macho culture, invite them to be compassionate, creative, in touch with their feelings, and comfortable with weaknesses and limitations.

The final issue I would like to address in this essay is the actual manner in which Hispanics understand spiritual direction. In my experience I have found three interpretations of what this relationship can be:

- Formal, individual spiritual direction
- Group spiritual direction
- Informal spiritual direction

By formal spiritual direction I mean the traditional meeting of director/ directee on a regular basis. I have found that it is usually middle- or upper-middle-class Hispanics who take advantage of this style of direction. Those who have a higher education, especially from Catholic schools, are also more open to this opportunity.

The second category is very common in my ministry. I have named it group spiritual direction, and it covers a myriad of experiences. Because of their extroverted nature, Hispanics are very open to group sharing. I have often found myself in the midst of a group of people who spontaneously begin to share with one another their spiritual journeys. When I engage in this ministry as a systematic process, it becomes a rich opportunity for the spiritual development of its members. In these situations among committed Christians, I have found an amazing willingness to share about their families and personal lives and an equally amazing openness to group discernment.

The last category is perhaps the most predominant of the three. I have called it informal spiritual direction. This experience includes people that meet with you for coffee after a meeting, who invite you to dinner and proceed to open up their souls to you, those who talk to you after or during a weekend retreat or in the midst of a family picnic.

For a long time I resisted the temptation to label this spiritual direction. Nevertheless, as the years pass, I have come to appreciate the value and richness of these encounters. In a way that I cannot explain, there is a connection established between a casual meeting and a follow-up conversation in a totally different setting two months later. Because of their ability to focus on the present moment, the director gets an honest and clear picture of the "now action" of God and can assist people to relate this event to their past and to be open to the future. Hispanics are storytellers, and the spiritual director has the challenge of connecting their individual stories with the story of Jesus.

The spiritual director with the Hispanic community is called to be a companion, a friend on the journey. She or he is expected to become almost a member of the family and to be an integral part of the directee's life. Somehow the spiritual director becomes a fellow pilgrim who has found the way yet continues traveling as a foreigner seeking a homeland.

13

Using Dreams and Imagination

BERNARD WARD, MCCJ

In cross-cultural spiritual direction, as in all spiritual direction, the director is first called to listen and be present to the directee. Effective listening, leading to trust, enables directees to tell their story, to relate their experience of life and find God in it. The use of dreams and imagination in cross-cultural spiritual direction is a helpful way of enabling directees to speak of their experience and work from their own culture. This article gives examples drawn from retreat work among black people in South Africa. The examples are used with permission and names are changed.

Central to the spiritual direction relationship is trust. Carl Rogers writes that, "In a wide variety of professional work ... it is the quality of the interpersonal encounter which is the most significant element in determining effectiveness ... which releases or promotes development or growth."[1] This is equally true of the spiritual direction relationship, where the quality of the relationship is the basis for the directee's growth in relationship with God. Thus it is a basic requirement that the directee be able to establish a deep level of trust. Trust puts the directee at ease and allows dreams to surface and the imagination to work freely. This is not to imply that the director does the work. It is to say that the trust that develops between the two people is the felt presence of the Holy Spirit, who guides the work.

Carl Rogers speaks of three "core-conditions" necessary for an effective counseling relationship: congruence, empathy, and unconditional positive regard. In the context of spiritual direction, the director uses these core conditions to establish a relationship of trust with the Lord. Thus congruence is the director being genuine in front of the directee, without posing but being himself or herself. Empathy is the ability to sense what the directee is feeling, though not necessarily alluding to the feeling until it is appropriate. Empathy is also the ability to place oneself in the directee's shoes, or to see things as the other sees them.

Unconditional positive regard might also be described as respect. In the spiritual direction context, respect is allowing directees the experience of being accepted by someone of another culture in such a way that they can experience themselves as being respected and loved by God. Thus cross-cultural spiritual direction mirrors the relationship between the directee and God.

The establishment of trust enables directees to begin telling their story and perhaps to speak of some experience for the first time, thus releasing potential for growth in their relationship with the Lord.

Mary, a black sister, was able to use her dreams and her imagination in prayer to heal hurts and to grow. In her first interview Mary described how she had been very badly treated at home. She and her younger sister, who had been placed in the care of her relatives, were very often beaten and starved. Her mother worked away and rarely came to visit them. During this time Mary made three attempts to take her own life by preparing poison. On each occasion she was prevented from drinking the poison when she heard a voice from behind her which gently called her name. Later, when she planned to enter the convent, her mother returned and beat her, breaking three sticks in the process. Part of Mary's reason for entering the convent was a dream of the same voice calling her.

This story and the pain it contained was told during a short preached retreat. Six months later Mary returned to make an eight-day directed retreat. As a Scripture text for prayer, I suggested she use Luke 12:22–32 on providence, praying on God's care for her during her life. The following day Mary presented two dreams. In the first she had met a man standing in a field showing her all the beauty in it and saying that she was just as beautiful. The voice of the man was the same as the one in her earlier dream calling her, and it was the voice that had saved her from suicide. This time it was not quite as soft, but it was the same.

In her second dream Mary found herself at the side of a wide river that she was unable to cross. This river had then come into her prayer. In her imagination she saw Jesus cross the river while she waited for him without going across herself. At the end of this session, I suggested she pray on Revelation 1:1–16, the man whose voice was like the sound of the ocean, and John 1:35–39, the call of the first disciples, which she was to pray as an imaginative contemplation. She was encouraged to use her imagination to place herself in the gospel incident and allow herself to become involved in the action, asking to come close to Jesus and to get to know him.

In the report of her prayer on the following day, Mary felt that the Revelation text had not been much help. However, in praying with John she found that Jesus lived in a desert. He sat and looked at her and she looked at him, and he loved her. For her next prayer we agreed on Mark 1:45 (Jesus had to stay outside the town in a lonely place where nobody lived), and a repetition of her prayer of sitting and looking at him. In the next directing session Mary reported that in her prayer she returned to the image of the river. This time she had been able to cross it and meet Jesus on the other bank. The following day found her wanting to touch Jesus and wanting to be touched by him. She wrote a prayer to this effect. She agreed to pray Mark 5:25–34, the woman who touches Jesus, and Mark 10:13–16, Jesus blesses children. In the next session she reported that in her prayer Jesus had touched her, saying, "Why did you wait so long!"

Following this Mary asked for a second interview later in the day, during which she could talk about her present relationship with her relatives. She usually spent her holidays with them and found this unbearable. No one in her religious community knew of her family situation or of the pain she had suffered as a child. In this meeting Mary came to the conclusion that she did not have to go on holiday to her godparents, but could go and stay at the mission nearby.

The dreams and images that Mary presented led to a closer meeting with Jesus. She was able to grow in confidence in his presence. At the same time the encounter with him in her prayer enabled her to grow as a person and to make a responsible decision about changing the relationship with her relatives.

Esther, a nurse, came on retreat feeling unwell and shaken by the recent death of a woman in the hospital where she worked. On the second day of her retreat, after praying Isaiah 43:2, you will pass through fire and water, Esther presented a drawing of herself walking through fire. She felt that she had already been through fire in the loss of her cousin and uncle in recent violence in Soweto. In the close-knit context of her culture, she and her cousin were like brother and sister, and her uncle had been a father to her since her real father had left home. Praying over a passage from Zephaniah (3:17: "He will exult with joy over you") helped Esther to sense the Father holding her and strengthening her, for her own sake as well as for the sake of those she nursed. From this position of trust in the Father, Esther moved into praying several gospel passages as imaginative contemplations.

After praying the walking on the water in an imaginative way, Esther presented the following dream. She is going on a journey and is given the choice of traveling by plane or by boat. Since she has never sailed, she decides to take the boat. Next she sees a woman floating in water who starts to drown and calls for help. Esther becomes the woman and feels herself drowning and calling for help. Help arrives and she wakes up.

Esther could make very little of this dream. Talking around it with her, I suggested that perhaps it was about trust and letting go, and particularly about trusting herself in a relationship with Jesus. She was setting out on a journey of faith with him, beginning a relationship and allowing herself to be helped. I felt too that there could possibly be something about her sexuality and her fear of it, all of which kept her from a deeper relationship with Jesus. However, I did not allude to this. I felt, though, that it gave an indication of where to go in the prayer. I suggested that Esther pray on Psalm 42:7 (deep is calling on deep), and that she pray on the woman taken in adultery and the anointing at Bethany as imaginative contemplations.

In the next meeting Esther described two dreams from the night before, one of a religious sister who is pregnant, and the other of her grandmother's funeral. She chose to speak about the funeral, saying it indicated a wedding, the opposite of death. Esther felt it might refer to her sister's, her niece's, or a friend's wedding. Since she did not bring herself into this dream, I asked how she felt Jesus saw her. At first she said he might see her as his sister, mother, or friend. Slowly she was able to say that he might see her as his lover or wife. Then very slowly, she described her imaginative prayer of the anointing at Bethany, moving her hands and caressing the air in a very sensual gesture of anointing Jesus' feet.

I suggested that Esther use passages from the Song of Songs in her next prayer. She had never heard of this book of Scripture. The following day found her very still and serene in her description of her prayer. From here she moved into praying the Passion, which again made her recall the death of her cousin and uncle. In this prayer she felt only loneliness and the pain of Jesus. At the same time she found herself able to forgive the police who had shot her cousin and left him in the street to die.

It is, I suggest, this movement into the Passion that shows that the movement indicated both by Esther's prayer and her dreams is the work of the Holy Spirit moving her deeper into a relationship with Christ. At the same time her ability to forgive is her felt experience of the Resurrection.

The dreams that Esther presented during her retreat gave indications about the direction to be taken in prayer. Similarly, those presented by Mary, linked with memories and dreams from the past, enabled her to sense the consistent caring action of Jesus in her life as expressed by the voice. The way in which the dreams of both women flow in and out of their life experience indicates that they are being true to their black culture in which all dreams have an important meaning and part to play. Clearly there are many other possible meanings that might be given to the dreams, but in the context of spiritual direction, the focus is on the link with prayer.

In the spiritual direction context, there seem to be five ways in which a dream can be used:

1. The directee can say what the dream brings to mind, such as a memory.
2. The directee can offer an interpretation of the dream: "For me the dream means this . . ."
3. The directee can say how the dream might be seen in his or her tradition, for example, a dream of eating would indicate that "I have been bewitched."
4. The directee or the director could interpret the dream in the light of

their relationship, or the directee's feelings about spiritual direction, for example, this dream seems to be saying, "I don't want to be here."
5. The dream can offer an indication of what is happening between the directee and the Lord, and be a sign of the directee's deep and unspoken desires in prayer, thus providing a guide for the direction to be taken in prayer.

Not all of these ways of looking at dreams can be used at the same time. On the whole, I feel the director needs to keep the focus on what the dream is saying about the directee's prayer and relationship with the Lord. The other possibilities should be noted and kept in mind. When a memory, an interpretation, or a deep fear presents itself very strongly, the director can suggest that the directee take this to the Lord in prayer, enter into conversation with him in an imaginative contemplation, and hear what he seems to say about it. Quite often when this is done, considerable insight and growth takes place and directees sense the Lord really working for them.

Although reference has been made to the importance of the core conditions of counseling and their importance in spiritual direction, spiritual direction is not therapy. During the retreat the director provides the "holding," enabling the retreatant to take risks in prayer, to explore unresolved issues with the Lord, and to risk greater intimacy with him. From time to time the director comes across a retreatant who is disturbed and more in need of therapy than a retreat. It may be necessary to suggest that the retreatant conclude the retreat. In some cases, though, the director may be able to provide the "holding" sufficient for the retreatant to conclude the week without feeling rejected, and sufficient for the directee either to gain the confidence to enter therapy or to maintain emotional boundaries until he or she can see a therapist. It is equally important that directors have worked on their own dreams and have had some experience of getting to know themselves through therapy. Likewise, the director needs to be in supervision.

When, as occasionally does happen, the imaginative prayer becomes very disturbed, unusually strange, violent, or becomes fantasy unconnected with the directee's relationship with the Lord, the director needs to suggest that the retreatant return to a quieter type of prayer, for example sitting with a psalm or passage from Paul and responding from the heart rather than the imagination. In such cases the director might even want to suggest a complete break from formal prayer, a day off, a long slow walk, or time spent looking, smelling, touching flowers and trees.

Not all directees bring their dreams or deepest hurts to a retreat. However, many do meet the Lord in the simplicity of their imagination. Martin had worked in the gold mines. Rather than meeting the Lord, he spent much of his prayer thinking, until he saw Jesus as a miner. Praying over the lines "come to me you who are over-burdened," Martin pictured himself working in the mine, carrying a heavy load. Jesus called him over to relax in a cool corner and offered him a drink of water. Martin noticed how Jesus smelt like a miner, and he felt that the smell united them.

Andrew, from a rural area in Kenya, imagined Jesus caring for the physical needs of the village, providing water and a road and being a person the villagers could really talk to. While praying the Passion, Andrew felt that Jesus had chosen a way of suffering to show the poor that their lives have meaning.

Eusebius, from Tanzania, found it difficult to imagine Jesus until he prayed the meeting between Jesus and Zaccheus and allowed the scene to take place in his own village. James, from a pastoral area of East Africa where cows are highly prized, began to sense God's love after watching cows graze and becoming aware of God caring for them. Albert felt particularly close to Jesus when he was able to imagine him entering Soweto on Palm Sunday.

In suggesting that retreatants pray with the imagination and picture Jesus in their own context, my hope is to enable directees to meet Christ as one like themselves rather than as a foreigner. An indication that a genuine encounter with Jesus has taken place is the movement into praying the Passion in a deeper way and the openness to meeting the Risen Lord in a different way, such as in the call to forgive or to value others from other races and cultures.

In cross-cultural spiritual direction, dreams and images can be a way of bridging the cultural gap. The image speaks where language fails. At the same time, the director is enriched by encountering Christ in many different ways. As one "coloured" South African said, "My Jesus speaks to me in many languages, and has many different faces."

NOTES

1. Carl Rogers, "The Interpersonal Relationship: The Core of Guidance," in *Person to Person* (Condor Souvenir Press, 1967).

14

Finding Identity in South Africa's Apartheid Society

GREGORY LOURENS

After the birth of a child, parents are expected to register the little person. In South Africa, you register your child according to the skin color, and that is the child's introduction to the apartheid system.[1] In a few days, when the child is taken home, the location of the baby's home is decided by the color of the parents' skin.

As the child grows up, it will begin to play with other children, and normally it will be children with the same skin color. When the child goes off to school, it will be placed in school according to skin color. After the child's education is completed, jobs will be open according to racial classification. Until recently, even a person's choice of spouse and where to be buried was determined by skin color.

Apartheid structures have affected everyone in South Africa. Not only are we confronted with these evil structures within our social and political lives, but worse, these structures have been internalized and now influence how we value and identify ourselves. Let me put this another way. If a person has "coloured"[2] skin in South Africa, that "coloured" skin makes the person a "coloured." If I have a "white" skin, then I am "white." I internalize the color of my skin, and my very identity and self-worth is forged from it.

The Church, together with other people of good will, has gone a long way to expose the evils of apartheid structures, and at the present moment the government itself has recognized these evils and is busy abolishing all remaining apartheid legislation. All of these activities and achievements have gone a long way to free all of us from this diabolical system.

But I feel strongly that we still have to address the internalized suffering caused by apartheid. If one's identity is not based on skin color, then what are the criteria by which we determine who we truly are?

I believe that spiritual direction is one important discipline that can address these internalized sufferings and can help a person find his or her true identity in God. To demonstrate this I would like to introduce you to a brave young woman who decided to take this journey through her sufferings into identity.

"You know, I have come to a point in my life where I really need help. I'm embarrassed to admit it, but I'm in a mess!" Rose whispered these words in a tired, depressed voice, but her eyes revealed her anxiety and near pain.

Rose sat in her chair; her oversized T-shirt with the portrait of Nelson Mandela seemed to swallow her up. "Here I am, head of the Justice and Peace Commission, employed by the Church to mobilize others to join the fight against apartheid . . . and I am no longer motivated myself . . . feel so guilty . . . out there people are dying for the cause, others are suffering and needing help . . . and all I can do is sit here and feel sorry for myself . . . shit, I am pathetic! How can I dare to pray if I can't even do my job any longer!"

A week later.

"I have been sitting with the Scripture you gave me . . . they are beautiful words . . . I had a strange dream last night . . . should I tell it to you? . . . Okay.

"Well, I dreamt that there was this beautiful swimming pool situated in the middle of a wonderful garden. The sun was shining brightly and all my friends were either playing in the pool or resting on the lawn. In the dream, as I watched this scene, I felt good; I just knew that I was the pool and that my friends were enjoying what I had to offer—refreshing cool water to drink, bathe, or play in. And all the while the sun shone down its blessings.

"But all of a sudden the pool began to change. Before my eyes the water began to disappear, and I became aware of huge black rocks lying at the bottom of the pool. They looked dangerous, and I was immediately grateful that none of my friends had dived deeper and damaged themselves against those dark monsters."

"Well, Rose, what do you think the dream is trying to say?" asked Paul, the spiritual director.

"Well, at first I just ignored it, but then while sitting in the bus coming over to see you, I began to think about it and the thought came . . . maybe God is showing me that I have those horrible rocks in my life . . . maybe he is showing them to me so that I can get them out before they hurt my friends or the people I work with!"

Paul sat and looked gently at Rose with a slight smile on his face. "Maybe there is another way of looking at that dream," he suggested.

"How?" asked Rose.

"Well, what struck me was that the sun was shining on the water-filled pool."

"Yes," replied Rose.

"Was the sun shining on the pool full of rocks?" asked Paul.

"Yes, it was. Actually the scene was exactly the same, except for the missing water."

"Well, how would it feel for you if I were to suggest that the sun shining down was the love of God shining down on you?"

"Wonderful!" replied Rose.

"And how does it feel if that same sun is shining down on the rocks?"

"You mean the love of God shining down on my rocks?" asked Rose, her eyes wide with shock.

"Yes."

"That's impossible . . . God does not love rocks."

"Well, the sun does not vanish when the rocks appear."

Rose sat in silence, the air electric.

"Rose, I would like to suggest that you take your dream to God in prayer and ask him how he feels about your rocks—whatever they might symbolize in your life."

One week later Rose came in and sat down. She was breathless with excitement. "A powerful thing happened to me when I took my dream to prayer. In my mind's eye I could see the pool and the rocks, and just as I was to enter into the presence of God, a little thought crept into my head— 'Hey, Rose why don't you sneak down into the pool before God comes and remove some of those bloody rocks?' That thought hit me real hard, and then bingo! The lights came on. Suddenly I realized that I am more interested in getting the rocks out of my life . . . becoming perfect . . . than I am in God. Actually, I realized my main reason for coming to see you is not to strengthen my relationship with God, as I initially said, but rather to fix myself up and become perfect."

Rose was silent for a long time. "Boy, that was one of the most humbling experiences of my life!"

"And what do you want now?"

"I see more clearly now that I really do want God. Before, I wanted to be a beautiful swimming pool. I wanted to be useful. I wanted to be relevant in South Africa. I wanted to be in the forefront in the overthrow of apartheid. I wanted to be admired.

"And I suppose that is why I am suffering from burnout . . . my need to please everyone—the bishop, the parish priest, my mother, the poor, the blacks. I am ashamed to admit that God has never really fitted into the picture, except to bless my efforts!"

Rose lowered her head and wept bitter tears of freedom.

"Rose, in the light of all that has happened, what do you want to do in this coming week?"

"I would like to stay with the dream. I want to give God a chance to shine his rays on me. I want to really experience those rays."

A week later.

"When I went to prayer this week, to my surprise, I found myself in the swimming pool with the rocks, and as I lay there I became aware of the sun shining on me, and very slowly I began to feel a warmth swell up within me. It was as if God was saying: 'Yes, Rose, I do love you. Feel my love. I love you, rocks and all.' I was all mixed up inside; I was tearful, full of wonder, and at the same time all sorts of doubts were racing through my head. I think I need to stay with these doubts and speak to God about them."

A few weeks later.

"Rose, you have been living with your dream for a few weeks now. I would like to suggest that we stop for a moment and try to evaluate what God has been doing in this time."

"For me it is clear: First, God caught me by the neck and has stopped me from trying to live out my great dream and need to be the savior of South Africa. Second, he has been teaching me to just sit still and allow him to be God and to love me. I just know that the rays of his love have reached deep down within me and have touched my very being!

"If I remember how burned out I was when I first came to see you and how I now feel, I feel like a different person. I feel so alive!"

"Rose, I would like to suggest that you meditate on Ezekiel 16:6–14 next week and keep in mind how alive you are feeling."

A week later.

"I am really wasting time coming to see you. All this meditation is a luxury only whites can afford. In the past week, eight of my comrades have died on the streets. I really think spiritual direction is designed to keep whites living in a comfortable spiritual vacuum. Man, if I am really honest, I have become more and more self-centered since I have been seeing you. I think you whites should stick together and pray the revolution does not blow up in your neighborhood."

"Rose, you seemed to have had a tough week?"

"Did you read the papers yesterday? They shot those kids in cold blood."

"I understand you must be really hurting, but before we discuss it any further, could I ask you if you looked at the Ezekiel passage?"

"I hated it!"

"What happened?"

"Well, as you know, I have been having a wonderful time with God, really enjoying his company. It was so wonderful. But then that bloody Scripture spoiled it all! Instead of staying with the passage as you suggested, my eyes moved up a few lines and I read about nobody being there to cut my navel-string, and I just began to howl. It was so painful."

Rose sat there tearing a tissue into small pieces while large tears streamed down her face.

"You don't know what it is like to be born a coloured in this bloody country. If blacks are second-class citizens, then I tell you coloureds are third or fourth in line! Nobody wants you. You are neither black nor white. My father is so disgusted with himself for being coloured that he just drowns himself in alcohol. So when I was born, my father just saw another bloody coloured lying there in her filthy blood! He just walked away and had another bloody drink. And me? I have been left lying there in my blood with nobody to cut my navel-string ever since." Rose's chest was heaving out the bitter anguish.

"Rose, I know this is going to be very painful, but I would like to suggest that you stay with the Ezekiel passage."

The following week.

"Every time I look at that passage, memories just crowd my mind. One particular memory has repeated itself a few times: I am very young, sitting with my brothers and sisters in the back of my dad's old car. He has gone into a shop to buy us cold drinks. I can see him at the counter asking for the drinks. The white woman behind the counter begins to scream and shout and wave her arms about. My dad backs off, leaving the drinks on the counter. He walks out of the shop without saying a word, his face a cloud of fury. When he climbs into the car, he mumbles something about the shop having run out of cold drinks and then drives home in an icy silence. My mother does not say a word. At home father disappears into the old shed to drink himself into a stupor, and my mother vents her fury on us by demanding we clean the yard. I did not really understand what had happened; all I remembered was my father backing away from the white woman as if there was something seriously wrong with him. And it is that feeling that has eaten into my very bones. There is something wrong with us. We are not white."

For the next few sessions Rose painfully recalled what it was like to be born a coloured in South Africa. Her emotions ranged from pain to blind anger to black futility.

"Rose, I would like to suggest that you take the birth of Jesus passage from Luke for contemplation—and please remember to contemplate it. Enter into the scene with all your senses and allow the Holy Spirit to take over and guide you in whatever way he might choose."

A week later.

"You are really going to think I am crazy when I tell you what happened to me this week. It was the weirdest, most wonderful experience of my life. I find it difficult to talk about. Well, I began the contemplation as you suggested, and it went along according to the Scripture. I saw Mary and

Joseph; I could hear the sounds of the donkey as it made its way to Bethlehem; I watched as they struggled to find a place for the night (I know what that feels like!); I could smell the animals in the stable. Then it was time for Mary to give birth to Jesus, and *bang* before I realized what was happening, I was the baby struggling to be born!" Rose was looking at me with big questioning eyes.

"Yes, and what happened then?"

"It was so real. I was being born. I was aware of light and the sounds, and my lungs frantically trying to breathe. Then I was lying there, and it was all over. Gradually I became aware of faces looking down at me. Mary, Joseph, and Jesus. But it was the way they were looking at me. It was with such joy! Their faces were welcoming me. They were saying, 'Rose, welcome into life; we see you; you are wonderful—WELCOME.' "

Her whole being was radiating a vital, dynamic joy. They sat smiling at each other for a long time.

"I don't want to move my meditation at the moment; I just want to stay in the stable."

The following week.

"This contemplation has taken on a life of its own! Yesterday I repeated the prayer, and this time I was lying there as the baby with all three looking down at me, when very gently, Mary picked me up and placed me into warm water and began to bathe me. I didn't realize I was still covered in blood. Well, anyway, as she cleaned me, I began to notice my own skin— my *coloured* skin. I began to scream, cry, curse, hit out, until eventually I collapsed exhausted into a shit heap. Our skin is the colour of shit, you know! Black is beautiful, white is pure, black is the future color of our land. Mary's skin was so white and pure. Mine is shit! Oh how I wished I was black or at least white!" Rose was panting for breath, the now-familiar tissue paper lying in shreds in her lap.

Rose continued to speak, but now in a whisper. "Then it began to happen. Mary knelt over me and began to kiss my body. There was not one part she did not kiss. I could feel her healing lips caress my skin. My skin, my whole being seemed to be in my skin, and she was kissing my coloured skin. She was kissing me! It seemed as though she kissed me for hours. My skin was alive and tingling—I was alive.

"Eventually, she dried me with a towel and gave me to Jesus. I lay in his arms, and he stroked me with his warm hand. As he did this, I began to remember all sorts of experiences of shame and humiliation I had lived through because of apartheid, and as I remembered them, Jesus seemed to stroke them away."

A week later.

"When I went home last week, I went to the mirror and had a good look at my face. I have a serious face; most people don't believe that I am still in my twenties. I suppose my face reveals what I have been looking at most of my life—suffering. It's a strong face, and I really like it!

"A few days later it was my mom's birthday, so I went round to be with the family. When I gave her my present, without thinking, I spontaneously hugged her. I am never physical with anyone, especially not my parents, and here I was hugging my mother! It was good, and I could not let go. I held my body against hers and began to melt—to let go. I began to howl, I cried and cried. It was as if all my resistances were melting and I was coming home to my mom, my family, my identity, and myself. I was no longer embarrassed to be a member of my family.

"When I walked home that evening, I felt so alive. I found myself either greeting or smiling at everyone on the street. Whether they were black, white, pink, or green, I greeted them, and most smiled back, and it was good to be alive and to belong to this human family. This is the first time I really feel that I belong, that I can take my place in God's creation. Before, I was the embarrassed, angry outsider always working my butt off trying to earn my way in."

"Rose, I would like to suggest that you now go back to the Ezekiel passage I gave you a few weeks ago and see if God wants to speak further."

A week later.

"The passage was so different this week. I felt the words 'live and grow like the grass of the fields' were being spoken to me. I find it difficult to believe that God is giving me permission to just live! Nobody has ever encouraged me to live, to grow, to become me. All the voices in my head tell me what to do or not do; none of them give me permission to simply enjoy being me!" Rose's whole being seemed to radiate vitality. She had a new haircut and a small daisy between her fingers.

"Yesterday I went to listen to Nelson Mandela. I really admire that man and the price he has paid for the poor. But you know, for the first time in such a meeting, I did not feel guilty or enraged because I was not doing enough for the cause. Rather, I was able to recognize that Mandela was doing his thing and I am to be me and do things my way.

"I think I need to stay with that Ezekiel passage a little longer."

A few weeks later.

"You know, this invitation to live is amazing. I am waking up earlier and enjoying the sounds of the birds in the morning stillness. I gave myself permission the other night to sit and listen to a friend's beautiful records—wonderful. I feel I have been missing so much.

"I have also been doing a lot more walking, especially after work. My favorite walk is through the park and watching the signs of fast-approaching spring. I so love the smell of damp earth; it reminds me of my childhood and sitting amongst my father's vegetables.

"But I am so grateful that you pointed out my misunderstanding concerning the rocks in my swimming pool. That was the turning point in my life. Boy, I really hated that rock labeled *coloured*. I tried to ignore it; I blamed everyone else for creating it, and I wanted to throw it at anyone within range. But what I was really trying to do was rid myself of a painful part of myself.

"In South Africa, whether I like it or not, for the time being I am seen as a coloured, and I had to come to grips with that reality. Over the past months, God has been loving me with my coloured skin and at the same time he has been teaching me to embrace and love myself. Now I can embrace my skin, and slowly I am daring to reach out to others with different skin colors. Color of skin has been so bloody important in this country and yet in the depths of our hearts we know we are brothers and sisters. If we are going to authentically embrace one another as family, we will first have to come to peace with ourselves.

"I am beginning to understand why relationships are so important to God. He wants us to enter into right relationship with ourselves, so that we can initiate right relationships with others. When we have right relationships, we have justice! And now I see more fully what my role will be in the Peace and Justice Commission!

"I was looking at the Ezekiel passage again. It was talking about breasts and hair growing, and I am wondering whether God is not wanting to speak to me about my sexuality."

When Rose (not her real name) first came for direction, she was in a state of serious burnout and depression. Her motivation for coming to direction was to seek God and God's assistance to overcome her "lack of motivation to do his will."

As I got to know Rose, it gradually became clear to me that her self-image and sense of self-worth were mostly dependent on how other people saw her, whether it was her mother, the bishop, or the people she was working with or for. She was driven to perform correctly, to be perfect in their eyes. In the same way, she was driven to please God. As a result, she had lost touch with her own physical realities and ended up in severe burnout and depression.

Initially all her energy in direction was centered around trying to overcome her physical and emotional "problems" so that she could return to normal and go out and perform once more. It was the dream that helped her to get in touch with her deeper self.

Before that, her sense of self was very limited. At a primal level she could not accept who she was. This denial of herself was due to the interconnection of two factors: her family and how they failed to value her, which was made more problematic because of apartheid and how it had influenced her parents and their own sense of self-worth.

Many people in South Africa knowingly or unknowingly are living out the identity that the apartheid system has given them. They passively submit and internalize the identity and self-value that the system incorrectly gives them. Maybe Rose's parents fall into this group of people. Others, like Rose, rebel against apartheid and want to be freed from its influence. A common way of doing this is to step beyond apartheid definitions: I am a human being. I will not define myself as a black, white, or coloured. Now this is all true, but as in the case of Rose, a person can intellectually come to these conclusions and yet on a deep inner level still be living out an emotional experience of being black, white, or coloured.

Rose hated apartheid and all it stood for and was actively involved with its downfall, but when she was confronted with her own skin in prayer, all the deep pain, humiliation, and anger surfaced, and it was only after she had embraced all of this and was loved and freed in it that she was able to accept and enjoy herself as a human being with a coloured skin.

Once this happened, Rose gradually began to develop a sense of herself as an individual not dependent on others and their opinions. She was free now to be herself and ready to work with God to free other victims of apartheid.

In reference to spiritual direction itself, I trust this case history illustrates how important it is to allow directees to situate themselves within their own given reality. Each directee comes from a unique background that was influenced by their family, education, and the type of society within which they grew up.

God speaks to us powerfully through Scripture, but God can speak just as powerfully through the directee's given reality. We as directors need to take their reality and experience most seriously. In so doing, we teach directees to respect their own experience and try to find God and what God is saying in it all. In this way the directee also begins to experience God as relevant and alive in this twentieth-century world.

I trust you noticed that in this case history I allowed the directee to choose what she wanted to speak about and to decide the pace at which we moved. I believe this gives people a growing sense of themselves and their co-responsibility to work out their salvation with God. If we do not do this, they will remain dependent upon us as their director.

NOTES

1. As this is being written in 1991, F. W. DeKlerk, State President in South Africa, is calling for the eradication of the apartheid laws, including registration by race, separate school systems, residential areas, and so forth. However, even when these laws are abolished, the psychological and spiritual harm of apartheid will linger long in the individual and collective psyches of South Africans.

2. In South African racial parlance, "coloured" refers to a mixed racial background. Often people will speak of "so-called coloured" persons as a way of criticizing apartheid's racial classifications.

15

Forming Spiritual Directors in Ghana

TERRENCE P. CHARLTON, SJ

"We are asking members of our local communities to offer spiritual direction to seminarians who will be living with them for two years of active ministry. Can you help us prepare them to do spiritual direction?"

"I found the directed retreat so helpful; can you suggest someone in my locale I could contact for spiritual direction?"

"I have people from our local prayer group coming to me with difficulties they are having in prayer. What do I tell them?"

"The sisters from the parish came to me the other day asking if I would give them a weekend retreat. What do I do?"

Out of our efforts to respond to such requests came the program we call "The Art of Spiritual Direction." From the beginning it has been a program in process, evolving and developing from what we learned as we went along. We, the staff of the program, will try to share this program and what it has taught us about helping persons grow as spiritual directors in a third world country.

The staff members of the program are drawn from the personnel of the staff of the Centre for Spiritual Renewal, Kumasi, in south central Ghana, a diocesan center that reaches out to all of Ghana in its ministry. We are one priest from England and three sisters and one priest from the United States, and each is from a different religious congregation.[1] All of us have received formal training in spiritual direction and have found that our diverse backgrounds in education, counseling, Scripture, and theology help us to make important contributions to the program.

Our first effort to develop spiritual directors in Ghana resulted in a six-day workshop that we offered three times between March 1987 and March 1988 to a total of thirty-eight persons. From the experience of these workshops arose the decision to develop a fuller program that would better help potential directors acquire the knowledge and develop the skills needed to engage effectively in this ministry.

THE PARTICIPANTS

We decided from the outset that the program should be open to qualified laity, religious, and priests. Questions arose regarding requirements, since we did not want to exclude potentially good directors because they did not have this or that "ideal" qualification for undertaking the program; yet we knew screening was necessary to insure that participants could benefit from the program. For example, should we require courses in theology? Should participants be in spiritual direction themselves in a country where there are so few directors available and where distances are great and travel difficult?

We finally decided to require a basic knowledge of psychology, spirituality, biblical studies, and theology, and six months of spiritual direction or a directed retreat of at least three days. Recognizing the importance of life experience, we also required that participants be at least twenty-eight years of age and have at least three years of work or ministerial experience. Lastly, we demanded a commitment to the program in all its aspects and an openness to sharing faith experience.

In order to screen participants we decided against a spiritual autobiography, because such an exercise would be unfamiliar to many and some qualified participants might be put off. A personal interview seemed impractical because of the difficulty of transport, and a telephone interview impossible because phones are unavailable in most parts of the country. Since letters of reference tend to be unhelpful here because the referees often have difficulty providing a useful assessment, we decided only to require a letter of reference from the diocesan bishop for a diocesan priest, from the pastor of their parish for a layperson, and from the major superior for a religious.

As we look to the future, we are concerned about more careful screening. Hindsight indicates that letters of reference would have been a more effective tool if we had requested assessment of the applicant from particular concrete perspectives, and also that a spiritual autobiography could have been effectively utilized if we had explained the contents of such an essay and had asked a series of specific questions to be addressed in the autobiography.

Twenty-six entered the program when it commenced in January 1989, along with the thirteen of those who had made an earlier workshop, for a total of thirty-nine. Of these, twenty-six completed the program in May 1990. Those who dropped out of the program did so because of scheduling difficulties with their work or unavoidable absences from the country. Table I shows a breakdown, according to several categories, of those participating in the program at its mid-point in October 1989.

TABLE I

CATEGORIES OF PARTICIPANTS AS OF OCTOBER 1989

		Women	Men
Religious (non-priests):	Ghanaians	4	1
	Other Africans	3	1
	Expatriates	7	0
Laity:	Ghanaians	0	1
	Expatriates	1	0
Priests:	Ghanaians	-	8
	Expatriates	-	6
	TOTAL	15	17

We generally found that Africans had fewer opportunities for academic work in such fields as psychology or theology than non-Africans. On the other hand, the Africans, especially the Ghanaians, had the distinct advantage of a better understanding of the culture. Religious usually had more experience with a variety of prayer forms than the others. The ease of participants in being consciously reflective about experiences varied a great deal from person to person, but it often seemed easier for non-Africans, we speculate, because such reflection is more a Western cultural value.

Participants were engaged in a wide variety of ministry. Our data indicated that the thirty-two participants at the midpoint of the program had the following as their primary ministry:

Pastoral and Catechetical Work	12
Teaching	5
Hospital Ministry	4
Spirituality Ministries	4
Early Formation for their Religious Congregations	7

In addition, two of those engaged in other ministries were also involved in formation work on a part-time basis.

PROGRAM DESIGN

The program itself became a series of four workshops spaced over a period of sixteen months followed by an internship in spiritual direction or retreat direction which could be completed in a variety of ways, either at the Centre for Spiritual Renewal or through the participant's ongoing ministry. The workshops were a full six days each, with arrival and an initial meeting on the evening before the first day and departure on the seventh day. Each of the four workshops was held twice, once at the Centre in Kumasi and again in northern Ghana.

Ongoing work between the workshops included reading *The Practice of Spiritual Direction* by William A. Barry and William J. Connolly[2] between Workshops II and III and *Spiritual Freedom* by John English[3] between Workshops III and IV. Anyone who had not made a directed retreat of eight days was required to make one before Workshop III. Between Workshops III and IV, each participant served in the role of spiritual director or in a helping role so that she or he could do two written verbatims of the sessions. These verbatims were to include evaluations of the sessions.

The understanding of spiritual direction operative in the program is that given by Barry and Connolly in *The Practice of Spiritual Direction.* They define Christian spiritual direction as "help given by one Christian to another which enables that person to pay attention to God's personal communication with him or her, to respond to this personally communicating God, to grow in intimacy with this God, and to live out the consequences of this relationship."[4]

We divided the material of the workshops into six categories, each of which concerns some essential aspect of the knowledge or skills a person needs in order to help another according to this understanding of spiritual direction. The categories are prayer, life journey, discernment and decision making, counseling skills, spiritual direction, and evaluation.

Table II gives an outline of the workshops according to these categories and can serve as a basis for our discussion of the workshops.

TABLE II
THE CONTENT OF THE WORKSHOPS

Categories	**WORKSHOP I**	**WORKSHOP II**
Prayer	Daily prayer experiences	Daily prayer experiences
	Daily personal prayer	Daily personal prayer
	Prayer as personal	and prayer partners
	relationship to God	Praying our experiences
	Praying with Scriptures	Patterns of development
	Review of Prayer	in prayer
	Images of God	Dryness
	Teaching others to pray	
	The contemplative	
	attitude and the	
	awareness examen	
Life Journey	Assessing my experience	Stages of psychosocial
	Journaling:	development
	Stepping stones	Journaling an experience
Discernment and	Basics of discernment	Discernment and Scripture
Decision Making		Principles of discernment
		and the will of God
Counseling Skills	Awareness of feelings	Problems with feelings
	Dynamic stages of	Stage II skills
	counseling	
	Listening skills	
	Stage I skills	

Categories		
Spiritual Direction	Meaning, scope, and purpose The initial interview What to do after the session The director: qualities and pitfalls Case Study Staff and participant modelings Triads	Case study Staff and participant modelings Triads
Evaluation	Individual and group evaluations of the workshop Individual sessions on personal weaknesses and strengths	Individual and group evaluations of the workshop Individual sessions on personal growth
Categories	**WORKSHOP III**	**WORKSHOP IV**
Prayer	Daily prayer experiences Daily personal prayer and prayer partners Retreat dynamics The Prayerful Person	Daily prayer experiences Daily personal prayer and prayer partners
Life Journey	Stages of faith development Overview of the Spiritual Exercises	Detailed study of the Spiritual Exercises Journaling: the dialogue
Discernment and Decision Making	Decision making in the daily life Ignatian Rules for Discernment	Witchcraft, dreams, and visions in discernment
Counseling Skills	Stage III skills Introduction to verbatims	Review of the three stages Effective use of the probe Review of verbatims
Spiritual Direction	Spiritual direction vs. pastoral counseling Follow-up on Barry & Connolly Triads	Scrupulosity and legalism Sexual issues in spiritual direction Staff modeling Triads
Evaluation	Individual and group evaluations of the workshop Individual sessions on future ministry in spiritual direction	Individual and group evaluations of the workshop Individual session on integrating the program into participant's work

We will consider materials that we took up in each category and what we discovered and learned. Obviously, some of the topics and exercises could be listed under more than one category. We strove always to use an adult model of learning, avoiding lectures as much as possible and working to draw out the rich experiences of our participants. For example, we often would give participants questions on a topic to ponder, have them share in small groups, and report to the assembly.

PRAYER

Prayer is essential to spiritual direction, both for director and directee. We emphasized that the director should be a prayerful person in order to be helpful to another in her or his spiritual growth. Therefore, in addition to considering particular topics regarding prayer, we also provided opportunities for prayer. We began each day with a fifteen-minute exercise that would expose participants to different forms of prayer. By Workshop III the participants rather than the staff took responsibility for planning and leading these prayer experiences under the guidance of a staff member. Instead of asking participants to find time for personal prayer on their own, we set aside a time for personal prayer in our schedule each day as a way of emphasizing the importance we placed on prayer for the spiritual director. We often suggested that participants pray over topics connected with material we had taken up during the day.

Beginning with Workshop II, we introduced the daily use of prayer partners. Each participant chose a prayer partner for that workshop. After spending forty-five minutes in prayer and fifteen minutes in reflection on prayer, participants spent thirty minutes with their partner, during which each shared his or her prayer with the other for fifteen minutes. When we introduced this exercise, many of the participants expressed discomfort because they felt unready to be spiritual directors for one another. We explained that the emphasis was on each person sharing the experience in prayer and the partner receiving it. The person receiving the experience of the other need make no comment. Our primary goal was to have potential spiritual directors become comfortable with receiving the intimate sharing of another's prayer. In fact, the exercise proved very effective in helping participants grow, not only in their abilities to listen and receive, but also to respond appropriately to another's experience in prayer.

One important topic that we considered in connection with prayer was images of God, since these images fundamentally affect an individual's relationship to God. Because much of the time these images are not brought to conscious awareness, it is important that the spiritual director be able to discern what images of God are affecting the directee and help the person bring them to conscious reflection.

For some, God is personal but very distant. There is the story in Ghana that a woman was pounding fufu (a traditional dish made from boiled cassava, yams, or plantain) and poked God in the eye with her long pestle, so that God moved far away from humans. For others, perhaps also influenced by traditional religion, God is an impersonal power. As a result, some are inclined to use prayer, fasting, or living a moral life as a means of magical manipulation of God. Because biblical fundamentalism (which is very prevalent in Ghana) often uncritically accepts some material in the Hebrew Scriptures that treats God as arbitrary or vindictive, such views of God are not corrected by Jesus' invitation to relate to God primarily as a loving parent.

One topic that we presented, "The Prayerful Person," arose from our experience of working with the participants. We found it important to help them reflect on the ways in which one can grow into a prayerful person and to make a distinction between "praying" and "saying many prayers." In many religious congregations in Africa, there is so much "required" prayer that there is neither the time nor the flexibility needed for one to grow in relationship to God through prayer. Participants need to reflect on prayer as relationship, not duty, and one of the ways in which human relationships grow and mature. In many congregations there is a need to reconsider the spiritual exercises prescribed by rule, to see if quantity has been substituted for quality.

LIFE JOURNEY

Because God's communication with us and our response takes place in the concrete situation of our lives, we also focused on "life journey" as a category of reflection and input. Several topics were designed to help participants reflect on and understand their experience in a developmental way. We spent a good deal of time in Workshop II on Erikson's stages of psychosocial development[5] and in Workshop III on Fowler's stages of faith development.[6] We thought that paradigms such as these were important for directors in understanding human experience and in realizing that there is a direction of growth in our experience. We found that we had to take care to avoid jargon and to relate material presented to the participants' own experience. They did role playing on the different stages to ensure that they understood the material as related to their experience. Although this material was new to most, we found that participants were generally quite receptive to thinking in terms of developmental stages. Several gained important insights about their personal experience and better understood the perspective of others. Ghanaians and other Africans were able to apply the stages to their own cultures.

As a means of understanding growth in the spiritual life, Workshop IV was structured around the Spiritual Exercises of St. Ignatius. We introduced the dynamics of the Exercises at the end of Workshop III and asked participants to read through English's *Spiritual Freedom* slowly and to use the Spiritual Exercises as a reference. We suggested that they use themes and materials from the Exercises for their prayer. In Workshop IV itself, we presented the Exercises as a paradigm for Christian conversion and for growth in relationship to God and growth in freedom. Preparing some participants to direct retreats was secondary to enabling all the participants to understand this growth through the Exercises. We presented particular texts in relationship to this dynamic of growth. If this movement is understood, it becomes easier to deal with culturally bound aspects of the text and see the place for suitable adaptation. We oriented as much of the material of Workshop IV as possible toward the movement of the Exercises. For example, we took up scruples on the day we were discussing the First Week, and we presented the journaling technique of dialogue in association with a discussion of colloquies in the Exercises.

DISCERNMENT AND DECISION MAKING

We also worked in the area of decision making and dealt with the place of discernment in this process. The importance of interior movements and their subtlety were stressed. Many participants tended toward a reification of the will of God as if it were a preexistent reality to be grasped, instead of an ever-unfolding process approached through such activities as considering one's life situation, dialoguing with God in prayer, and discerning spiritual movements.

In many situations there can be perspective behind what the directee is saying that the director needs to become aware of in order to help the person effectively. This is particularly true in our situation, where director and directee may be from different cultures or where, because of the clash of ideas and quickly evolving cultural situations, two persons from the same culture may have significantly different ways of looking at reality. For example, if a woman speaks about neglect by her husband, losing money, and the illness of a child, the issue behind all of this might not be whether God cares, as the director might surmise, but the fear that someone has put a curse on her.

Belief in witchcraft can also be a delicate problem that the spiritual director must handle. If the director appears simply to reject witchcraft, the directee might turn elsewhere, to someone who would be more helpful to her or him. We cannot give a treatise on approaches to witchcraft here, but part of the solution lies in taking the beliefs and experiences of the directee seriously and helping the directee test these beliefs against their faith in God in order to bring their life situation more under the protection and providence of God. A similar problem can arise when the directee has a strong belief that spirits influence our world to such an extent that they seriously interfere with our free activity.

Because Ghanaians tend to experience visions and the act of hearing stimulates their prayer, and because dreams are taken to be indications of God's will, it was important that we help the participants understand that these phenomena are matters for exploration and discernment. They cannot simply be taken at face value as sure indications of God's will.

COUNSELING SKILLS

In our work with counseling skills, we particularly stressed the importance of feelings. While appreciating and attending to feelings is often a problem for people, this is a particular problem for Ghanaians and other Africans, among whom feelings are often hidden and not shared. In most social situations, they are only expressed in oblique ways, especially the so-called negative feelings. Although it did not seem particularly difficult for participants to appreciate the value of feelings, making this appreciation operative by attending to and valuing their own feelings was more problematic. Moreover, facility at attending to the feelings of another and reflecting them back required much practice.

In order to present counseling skills in a systematic way, we adapted materials from *The Skilled Helper*[7] and from works by Joe Currie.[8] In Workshop I we presented an overview of the stages involved in an effective helping process, and we also spent time with exercises focused on the pre-stage of attending, which involves the director's being present to the directee and listening to him or her. Then we spent time on Stage I skills that focus on the director's empathetic expression of the feelings and content presented by the directee, in order to facilitate the directee's self-exploration.

Stage II skills taken up in Workshop II concentrated on helping the directee to a deeper understanding of his or her situation in relation to enlarged perspectives on the world, God, self, and others. Workshop II presented Stage III skills through which the director helps the directee choose and take appropriate action as needed. We used Workshop IV for refining the various skills of all the stages. The participants were at very different places in their abilities to utilize and integrate the skills.

One of our biggest frustrations was probably that, within the strictures of the workshops, we could not spend more time practicing the skills. In offering the program a second time, we might present the skills more slowly. For example, we could introduce pre-stage and Stage I in Workshop I, with more practice in Workshop II; Stage II in Workshop III; and Stage III in Workshop IV. We also found that we had to take care that we presented the counseling skills in a broad context of exploring experience and addressing issues, so that an inadequate understanding of spiritual direction as problem solving was not reinforced by our work with the skills.

SPIRITUAL DIRECTION

The area of spiritual direction in each workshop is the place in which we drew together all the areas we have been discussing. There were a few sessions on specifically spiritual direction issues, such as sexual issues in the direction experience. We utilized case studies and modeled spiritual direction sessions in which staff served as director and directee, and a good amount of time was spent analyzing these presentations. Because we wanted the participants to use real materials in their practice sessions, we recognized that our modeling had to use real personal situations which were not practiced beforehand.

Much time was given to sessions in which the participants learned and practiced the counseling skills and drew on materials that had been dealt with in the workshops. This was understandably a slow process of integration. If one day, for example, we examined dryness in prayer and the next day in practice a directee talked about experiencing a "desert," the director still might have difficulty drawing on the materials on dryness in responding to the directee.

The practice took the form of triads. One participant would be director, another directee, and the third observer; the three roles would rotate until each participant had taken each role. A staff member was also present to give feedback at as many triads as possible. In Workshop I the sessions were brief: The first was five minutes of practice and five minutes of reactions and feedback by director, directee, and observer. By the end of Workshop III and during Workshop IV, the sessions were twenty-five minutes of practice and fifteen of processing.

We asked the directees always to use real and current material from their lives. We learned that when directees fail to do this, and either the material is fictional or the incident or concern is from the person's past and largely resolved, the directee's feeling reactions are muted or not accurate to the content. The practice is then less valuable to the director and perhaps even confusing, because the feelings of the directee in the session do not match the content.

Using real materials obviously implied that the participants develop a high level of trust in one another so that not only whatever was shared would be reverenced and held in confidence, but also that the directors would summon all their resources to respond as well as possible.

We also asked some of the participants to model as director and directee before the whole group. We found it was important to choose some of the more advanced participants to undertake these modelings. The analysis of these sessions by the whole group of staff and participants was very rich and a good learning experience for all. In spite of the value of this kind of session, however, by Workshop III we decided to forego this exercise in favor of more practice in the triads.

We ran into several difficulties with the conceptualization of spiritual direction from the participants. One problem was a confusion between spiritual direction and pastoral counseling. Several times we had to consider the essential difference between the two: the former focusing on the person's relationship to God, even though every aspect of the person's life can be considered in terms of this relationship, and the latter focusing on particular aspects of the person's life that need to be resolved or where the person needs to grow, even though their relationship with God is also considered.

Another misunderstanding was to see spiritual direction as problem solving: If there was no problem, then there was no need for direction. We worked hard to help participants see that often enough, when the directee is dealing with a problem, it is something that cannot be solved and attempts on the part of the director to do so will only lead to frustration. Instead, the director needs to help the directee live creatively with the problem in the context of his or her relationship with God. It was important for us to emphasize that spiritual direction can be both a significant means to appreciating in new ways how God is involved in a person's life and an important help to a person's being able to respond to God more fully and deeply in their life.

There was also a tendency to view the spiritual director as an advice giver. This model of spiritual direction seems to have affinity with the wisdom figure or the elder in traditional Ghanaian and other African societies. Not surprisingly, in a traditional society where so much is determined for a person and there are few areas of freedom, the spiritual director as the one who helps the directee "fit in" and know how to respond can be an attractive model. In Ghana it is not unusual for the directee to begin by saying, "I have come to you for advice," or to end the explication of her or his situation with the words, "Please tell me what to do." In addition to falling into the role of advisor because it is culturally accepted, it is also easy to do so because it is simpler to treat the situation in an objective way and to think: "If I could only understand the situation well enough, I would know what the person should do," rather than to deal with the complexity of the person in her or his uniqueness.

It is proper to ask whether we are forcing a contemporary Western model of spiritual direction onto a situation that is not ready for it, particularly when we realize that the spiritual director has been understood as a spiritual advisor in the Christian tradition. We confidently respond that Ghana is quickly evolving from a traditional society into a modern one that is much more complex and offers many more options. In fact, the model of spiritual direction that will best serve the Church and particularly Christians is one that helps each appreciate her or his special personal relationship with God and make choices in a way that considers the unique person one is before the God who calls each into the future.

PARTICIPANT EVALUATION

A final aspect of each workshop, participant evaluation, proved to be important to the development of the program and of the spiritual directors. At the end of each workshop the participants were asked to give some written feedback on what they had experienced in those six days, and there was some time for oral feedback in the group. As each workshop concluded, time was allotted for each participant to do a personal evaluation that was shared in a conference with a staff member who also gave feedback from the whole staff on the progress of that person.

The focus of Workshop I was on the strengths and weaknesses of the participants and what was needed for growth; in Workshop II it was the continued growth of the participant. Workshop III concentrated on the work the participant envisioned doing in the field in the future and whether the person should choose the specialized internship in retreat direction. We asked the participants to apply what they had been studying regarding a process of discernment to this choice. In Workshop IV the focus of evaluation was on integrating the learnings of the program into the participant's ministry.

INTERNSHIPS

As this article was being completed, we have just finished giving Workshop IV twice, so we cannot assess the internships but only discuss what we envision. We plan to have two internships: The one in spiritual direction is for all participants, and the other in individually directed retreats is for those for whom the participant and the staff agree it would be beneficial.

During the internship in spiritual direction, one staff member will work with each intern, who will prepare verbatims. The two will meet at regular intervals to discuss the verbatims. Audio recordings of the sessions used for the verbatims is encouraged. The frequency of meeting, the number of verbatims to be taken up at each meeting, and the length of the internship will be worked out on an individual basis between staff member and intern.

The internship in retreat direction will focus on preparation in directing the Ignatian retreat. Ten participants will make this internship, which will begin with a six-day workshop on this kind of direction. During the workshop, half of the interns will each spend two days directing another intern in a private retreat and will meet with a staff member for supervision on each of these days. During the subsequent two days, the roles will be reversed. Interns will then direct two- to three-day retreats under supervision. On the basis of ongoing evaluation, the intern will progress to directing longer retreats of up to eight days under supervision and finally to directing on her or his own. We will arrange this supervised direction of retreats both at the Centre in Kumasi and elsewhere in Ghana.

PROGRAM EVALUATION

We have attempted to speak of problems we have encountered and of what we have learned over the course of our program, but a few points remain. In the program and in all of our ministry at the Centre, we emphasize working as a team. We were surprised, however, at how many of the participants remarked that our teamwork is a model for ministers, particularly a group of women and men, working together as a team of equals. Aspects of teamwork that are noted are attending one another's presentations with the expectation of learning from one another, complementing and supporting one another, and our obvious enjoyment in working together. Such a witness is not something that we would have thought of planning, but it has helped participants envision the Church and ministry in new ways.

What is our overall evaluation of the program? Probably the most important measure we can give is that we have already scheduled the program to begin again in 1991. Much has been far from ideal, but given the limitation of the situation in the country, we judge that we have been successful in supporting the development of several of our participants as spiritual directors and as directors of individually directed retreats. Some participants have concluded that they are not presently called to engage in the ministry of spiritual direction, but that the knowledge and skills they have gained can be incorporated into their present ministries. Our experience continues to affirm us in helping to develop spiritual directors, a ministry which will be increasingly important for the growth of the Church in Ghana.

NOTES

1. At the time of writing of this article, the members of the staff in addition to myself are: Sr. Mary Anne Hoope, BVM, Sr. Germaine Maurer, SSJ, Sr. Patricia McAleese, PBVM, and Fr. Michael Targett, M. Afr.

2. William A. Barry and William J. Connolly, *The Practice of Spiritual Direction* (San Francisco, Calif.: Harper & Row, 1982).

3. John English, *Spiritual Freedom* (Guelph, Ont.: Loyola House, 1974).

4. Barry and Connolly, p. 8.

5. Development of Erikson's theory can be found in his books and articles, including the following: Erik H. Erikson, *Childhood and Society* (New York: W. W. Norton, 1950); *Identity, Youth and Crisis* (New York: W. W. Norton, 1968); and *Insight and Responsibility* (New York: W. W. Norton, 1964).

6. James W. Fowler, *Stages of Faith* (San Francisco, Calif.: Harper & Row, 1981).

7. Gerard Egan, *The Skilled Helper* (Monterey, Calif.: Brooks/Cole Publishing Company, 1985).

8. Joe Currie, *The Barefoot Counsellor* (Bangelore, India: Asian Trading Corporation, 1988) and *In the Path of the Barefoot Counsellor* (Bangelore, India: Asian Trading Corporation, 1986).

16

Toward a Multicultural Approach
to Spiritual Direction

JUDETTE A. GALLARES, rc

My interest in developing a multicultural approach to spiritual direction began twenty years ago when I experienced, for the first time, what it is like to leave one's own culture and insert oneself in a totally different one, the American culture, in my case. I had to go to the United States for my religious formation because at that time the congregation I was entering had no local formation house in the Philippines.

During the various phases of my formation, my formators and spiritual directors were all Americans. The process of acculturation to two cultures—the American and that of religious life—was an extremely difficult one. Although I had tried to familiarize myself with the American culture prior to entering, the shock was still tremendous. I felt uprooted from my own culture and people, from my native food, language, and even patterns of affection. Because there was so much I did not understand in the American culture, I felt insecure.

The whole approach to spirituality was somehow foreign to me. It offered me an integration that was mainly yang (masculine, linear, categorized, left brain, and Western), while my own experience was characteristically yin (feminine, circuitous, wholistic, right brain, and Eastern). I had difficulty articulating what was happening within me to my spiritual director and to the novitiate staff, for I was not sure where I stood with them. I kept reassuring myself that what I was undergoing was simply part of the normal process of adjustment to a new culture.

To make matters worse, I found English to be an inadequate medium for expressing my feelings. Although I had studied English in school and could speak it proficiently, I had never had to speak it all the time. I realized that my problem was that I was not used to *thinking* in English. The experience was draining, emotionally and physically. Once I was adjusted to the new culture, however, I realized that there was much that Western, specifically American culture, could offer for my personal and spiritual growth. At the same time, the opportunity to view my culture from a distance and from an objective perspective gave me a deeper appreciation of its strengths as well as its weaknesses and a better understanding of its development and positive and negative influences.

Ten years later, when I returned to my country to undertake the primary ministry of my congregation—retreats and spiritual direction—the experience of having to cross cultures proved invaluable. It still does.

At our retreat house, I constantly find myself called upon to direct retreats for people from various Asian cultures. (Our sisters are also invited to give retreats and other programs in other East Asian countries.) Even in ministering to people of my own culture, regional and socioeconomic differences demand that I cross certain barriers and subcultures. Thus my cross-cultural experiences have become more frequent.

In returning to my culture and in encountering the cultures of my directees, I realized that the education and training I had received in theology, spirituality, pastoral counseling, and spiritual direction were too Western and American. I needed to adapt what I had learned to suit the Filipino and Asian temperaments and to be relevant to the Asian culture. In doing so, I had to reinsert myself in my own culture to rediscover its unique gifts as well as flaws. I also had to learn to listen to the personal experiences of my directees as well as to the cultures that shape and condition their consciousness and responses to life. Moreover, I had to be constantly aware of my own listening, which could become complicated, especially if the frameworks that inform my listening no longer give adequate form to what I am hearing and thus get in the way of my presence to the directee. As a spiritual director, I have to be ever conscious that my first task is to listen.

My experience leads me to the conclusion that spiritual directors are called upon to listen not only to the person but also the culture that serves as a medium through which one perceives, experiences, lives, and expresses the very reality of one's faith. It implies that spiritual directors need to develop a global and multicultural view of the human situation. Given the complexity of the human condition in today's world, it is not sufficient that they are grounded only in theology, missiology, and Christian spirituality. The "signs of the times" challenge them to be critically informed by philosophy and psychology, as well as by sociology and anthropology.

EDUCATION OF SPIRITUAL DIRECTORS

My cross-cultural experience is only a small indication of the magnitude of globalization and cultural interdependence. Through sophisticated means of communication and transportation, the world has increasingly become one small global village. Given this reality and the global outreach of everything today, not just in religion but more increasingly in the socio-economic and political fields, it is imperative that church ministries, including retreats and spiritual direction, must be responsive to the signs and needs of the times. The exigencies of today's world challenge everyone, especially those in the helping ministries, to be inculturated, multiculturally aware, and skilled in multicultural communication in order to keep pace with people's changing consciousness and expanding horizons.

Consequently, the dynamics of spiritual direction are affected by divergent ways of thinking and orientation, of experiencing reality, of understanding one's personhood, and of communicating one's self between the Eastern and Western cultures of the world. What kind of educational program does the ministry of retreats and spiritual direction need to be relevant and responsive to today's multicultural world? What areas and questions must be addressed and raised in developing an ongoing program of education for spiritual directors?

I hope to address these questions and needs and to offer suggestions based on my experience, study, and interaction with those who have dealt with cross-cultural or multicultural situations. I shall discuss three main areas that I think are important in developing such a program: inculturation, multicultural psycho-spiritual processes, and multicultural awareness and communication.

My intention is not to offer a detailed structure or plan, but rather to ask questions, surface issues, and provide examples of emerging answers and directions, hoping these will serve as guidelines in the planning of an ongoing program of education for retreat and spiritual directors. I presuppose that the participants of the program have some theological, scriptural, and psychological background and previous training and experience in either pastoral counseling, retreat work, or spiritual direction.

INCULTURATION

Culture is the medium through which the very reality of human existence, faith, community, Church, and so forth can be perceived, experienced, lived, and expressed. Thus the way people perceive truth, interpret meaning, and understand their experience of reality is bound up with their particular context and tradition. While the primary focus and content of spiritual direction are the directee's relationship with God in his or her everyday life, this needs to be nourished and nurtured not only by prayer, but also his/her understanding of the meaning and content of faith as revealed through Scripture, the traditions, and the Church in the context of his/her present personal, familial, social, and cultural situation. In other words, being a Christian is not an abstraction but a contextual reality. And for the Christian message to have any relevance to people's lives, there must be inculturation.

What is our understanding of inculturation? What bearing does it have on spiritual direction? What are its implications on the practice of spiritual direction and on the training of spiritual directors? To answer these questions, let us first look at how inculturation has evolved as a theological process.

Theologians have agreed that for the past two decades since the Second Vatican Council, there has been a growing need and consciousness in the Church, especially in the churches of the third world, to adapt Christianity and its theological reflection to local circumstances in order to make sense of the Christian message. The word *inculturation* has emerged as one of several terms theologians have coined in their attempts to approximate the meaning of this shift in perspective. Inculturation came to be understood as "the dynamic relation between the Christian message and culture or cultures; an insertion of the Christian life in a culture; and an ongoing process of reciprocal and critical interaction and assimilation between them."[1]

With this new understanding comes a new sense of Christian identity that is emerging apart from much of the traditional theological reflection of historical Christianity. This new identity, according to theologian Robert Schreiter, is particularly sensitive to three areas: context, procedure, and history. In other words, inculturation calls for the following process in theological reflection: 1) an examination of the context in which the Christian message is brought, such as people's traditional ways and customs or the country's sociopolitical situation; 2) greater attention to procedures resulting from one's awareness of how context shapes reflection or how it gives urgency to questions and shape to answers (i.e., foreign procedures and ways of dealing with situations must not be imposed; they must emerge from the context itself); and 3) an awareness of the ambiguities of history — how it leads to a transformation of the present and to a reconstruction of one's understanding of the past.[2]

In helping the directee make sense of the Christian message in the context of the latter's relationship with God in everyday life, the spiritual director, as a bearer of the Christian message, must have an inculturated approach to theology. In his or her aim to help in the wholistic growth and transformation of the directee, she or he must be particularly sensitive to the latter's context, procedure, and history.

Therefore I suggest that any educational program for spiritual directors consider the following issues and questions that have an influence on the development of people's spiritual life. They are grouped under two general areas: resources of Christian and non-Christian theologies in the region's diverse histories and cultures, and symbols, myths, and images that shape a culture's consciousness and identity.

Resources of Christian and Non-Christian Theologies

In the diverse histories and cultures of a country or region, what are the resources of Christian and non-Christian theologies that have influenced people's spirituality and the practice of their faith? How can these be used to deepen people's faith life? For instance, there are elements in both Christian and non-Christian Asian prayer that have points of convergence. They are not necessarily alien to one another. One of these is the concept of "emptiness." Susana Jose, in her book *San Juan de la Cruz Today*, describes the richness of this concept in both Christian (through Christ's kenosis or self-emptying) and Buddhist spiritualities:

> The kenosis of Christ as a way of spirituality is directly related to self-sacrifice or an oblative love; or a deepened sense of mystery which becomes the very presence of God in one's depths. It becomes the hallmark of a holy and virtuous, totally surrendered life.
>
> It is ultimately in this sense that Buddhist emptiness which is fullness or "emptiness infinite" becomes not negative but positive spirituality.
>
> But in terms of actual prayer experience, both Christian and Buddhist impressions of "meaningless" and "thoughtless" contemplation are legitimate. The difference lies in the process of achieving that state.[3]

The challenge to spiritual directors today is to make creative use of existing resources in spirituality, whether Christian or non-Christian, in guiding people to God.

Symbols, Myths, and Images

God has many faces in Asia, the cradle of the world's great religions. In this region's multifaceted religiosity, the people's cosmic and animistic beliefs and practices have been assimilated into Hinduism, Buddhism, Islam, and Christianity. What are the clusters of symbol-images and myths that shape the thought, consciousness, and action of women and men in the societies and culture of a country or region today? What are the functions of symbols and myths in mediating religious experience and people's struggle for cultural identity? What are the culture's images of God and peoples' images of Jesus? What is the various cultures' theological world of symbols and images in which God and the human are engaged in a struggle for human liberation and salvation? I am aware that this last question might not be applicable to all cultures and religions; for example, the engagement between God and the human in people's struggle for liberation would be foreign to Buddhism, or the struggle for human liberation would be anathema to some cultures of Iranian descent.

We can begin to form the answers to these questions by learning to listen to the people's folk language, which is a rich deposit of the culture's wisdom and spirituality. Asian theologian Aloysius Pieris, SJ, once wrote that to grasp the language and symbol of a particular culture, one must "learn first the folk-language. Assist at their rites and rituals; hear their songs; vibrate with their rhythms; keep step with their dance; taste their poems; grasp their myths; reach them through their legends."[4] Perhaps we can adapt his suggestions according to our needs and situation and expand our understanding of it through examples. (These ways and experiences could be made available to spiritual directors as part of their training in inculturation.)

To participate or assist at people's rites and rituals. Here we are challenged to learn from the way people practice their faith. "Popular religiosity" or "folk religion" is one enduring manifestation of a culture's existing spirituality. Schreiter once commented that in the second period of the development of liberation theology in Latin America, liberation theologians realized their grave mistake in excluding folk religion. They realized that without an understanding of the folk religion of the peoples of Latin America, one would not know how the people coped with oppression over a period of centuries, nor did one know what resources the people, who were the subjects of the liberation process, had for liberation.

The same comment could be made about the Filipinos during the fateful four days of the 1986 revolution, when they faced danger and death. They fell back on a folk type of spirituality, leading many a theologian to comment that if the element of religious faith as manifested in the people's folk religiosity is excluded from any analysis, the experience of the people-power revolution cannot be grasped.

Certainly deep spiritual resources can be gleaned from people's religious practices. For instance, in the Philippines the Lenten season, especially during Holy Week, is full of rites and rituals. According to Filipino theologian Vitaliano Gorospe, SJ, "It was the native creative imagination and artistry of the village folk that transformed the four Gospels of the Passion of Jesus Christ into something truly distinctively Filipino."[5] He describes the four ways Filipinos use the Passion:

(1) *pabasa* (solemn reading of the *Pasyon*), with the Filipino addition of *pagkain* and *inumin* (food and drink for the devotees); (2) *kalbaryuhan* (outdoor re-enactment of the Way of the Cross and Calvary); (3) *sinakulo* (dramatic Passion play from the Cenacle to Easter, all throughout Lent); (4) *tapatan* (leveling) or *panawagan* (calling), both in the form of *bugtungan* (riddle-rivaling or contest).[6]

Spiritual directors need to be attentive to folk religions, especially if they are directing people who come from the grassroots, for these provide the context for constructing a more relevant local theology and for understanding people's spiritual journey.

To listen to peoples' songs, hear the culture texts, and vibrate with their rhythms. The metaphors and symbols contained in the lyrics and in the music often reveal the way people perceive themselves. For example, the words and poignant melody of a Filipino song about a bird with the capacity and freedom to fly, but which can cry only if imprisoned in a cage, expresses not only the true sentiment and hope of the Filipino people at a time of religious and political repression, but also their centuries of experience with foreign domination.

To "keep step" with people's dance and gestures. Folk dances and body gestures are rich expressions of a people's unique culture. They depict customs, traditions, and the way of life of a particular area or region. Gestures also convey cultural values and meanings. For instance, in the Philippines one shows respect for an elder person by asking his or her blessing. This is done by taking the elder's hand and putting it on one's forehead.

To "taste" the people's poems. For example, the poem of Korean Kim Chi Ha, who was tortured and imprisoned for his work in human rights, expresses the collective hope and aspiration of the people of South Korea at a time of political turmoil. The poem is entitled "Heaven Is Rice." The very title itself speaks of the Korean (Asian) people's spiritual aspiration (heaven) through the symbolism of a common staple food of Asia (rice). Although much of the poem's flavor has been lost in the translation, the "Eucharistic" message it carries is truly Asian. The poem goes this way:

> Heaven is rice
> As we cannot go to heaven alone
> We should share rice with one another
> As all share the light of the heavenly stars
> We should share and eat rice together
> When we eat and swallow rice
> Heaven dwells in our body
> Rice is heaven
> Yes, rice is the matter
> We should eat together.[7]

To grasp their myths and legends. For example, the concept of God as Creator is found in pre-Christian Philippine creation myths. These myths in fact would seem to be an improvement on the Genesis account, as they focus on the superiority of the brown race and the equality of man and woman.[8] The egalitarian concept can be gleaned from the various Filipino languages that use the same word for "him" and "her," "he" and "she," "brother" and "sister," and so forth. Unfortunately Christianity, with its colonial and male chauvinistic trappings, has downgraded this innate Filipino belief and concept of self.

An inculturated spiritual director could help the directee reclaim the spiritual resources of his or her past and realize that his or her culture not only receives the Christian faith but also enriches it.

To enter into their humor and laugh with the people.[9] Jokes can reveal a culture's or a person's concept or image of self and God. As a coping mechanism, jokes are a human way of dealing with the incomprehensibility of one's situation. Through humor, one learns perspective on one's life. For example, the jokes that went around town during the oppressive years of dictatorial government in the Philippines humorously depicted the kind of final judgment meted to the dictators in the afterlife. The jokes were a reflection of the culture's image of God and Divine Justice.

Other Inculturation Processes

There are many other ways of aiding the inculturation process. One that has been recommended for persons entering a new culture is the "immersion" or "exposure" program. The participant lives for a certain period (from two weeks to six months) with the people in a particular area, primarily as a learner, perhaps among the rural or urban poor. The program has the following features: orientation before the actual "immersion" experience; reflection with the people, as in the basic ecclesial communities; the participant's personal reflection with the program director; and evaluation of the experience at the end of the program. Such programs have been designed in third world areas such as the Philippines, where, for example, the La Ignatiana Apostolic Center regularly offers this experience to different groups and individuals, depending on need.

Other aids to the inculturation process are workshops, seminars, or courses on the different models of contextualizing theology and on the various ways and methods of prayer and spirituality.

The inculturation process would not be wholistic without the psycho-spiritual dimension of the culture. This brings us to the second area of concern in planning training programs for spiritual directors—the psycho-spiritual processes in multicultural situations.

MULTICULTURAL PSYCHO-SPIRITUAL PROCESSES

In the summary of the discussions of the 1988 FABC (Federation of Asian Bishops Conference) All-Asian Conference on Evangelization in South Korea, the following comments and observations were made on the emerging priorities and perspectives in Asia:

> In trying to find out the original genius of a people, we will have to study their values, their psychological orientation of mind, their mental slant, their priorities, their preferences and even their prejudices. In this effort to define the original genius of the Asian people, to discover the soul of Asia, I will not be wrong if I were to say that it is something of mystic reality.[10]

Since the ministry of retreats and spiritual direction is concerned with the conversion and transformation of the total person, those involved in the ministry should have adequate knowledge in dealing with the psychological and spiritual processes of the people to whom they are ministering. The worlds of depth psychology and religion lie close together and must endlessly seek to learn from each other. If there are as many ways of understanding personhood as there are different worldviews, there are also as many ways of misunderstanding personhood as there are worldviews. These need to be considered in mapping out the direction of the multicultural program for spiritual directors.

In this regard, certain questions and concerns demand further attention. These can be grouped under the following areas: individuation/differentiation processes; "transference" and "counter-transference" in the multicultural situation; and possible alternatives to the one-on-one structure of spiritual direction.

Individuation/Differentiation Processes

The notion of "self" is interpreted and understood differently in every culture and society. Psychologist Alan Roland, in the cross-cultural studies he has done in India, Japan, and America, has found that the intrapsychic self varies significantly, if not radically, according to the social and cultural patterns of societies so different in civilization. He has established that "people have different experiential, affective senses of self and relationships, as well as vastly different internalized world views that give profoundly different meanings to everyday experience and relationships."[11]

What then is the particular culture's notion of self? What is the individuation process of the Asian person (Japanese, Korean, Indian, Filipino, and so on) as compared to that of the Westerner? What is the psychology of the "familial self" as opposed to the psychology of the "individual self"? How is the self differentiated in the Asian family system? Considering the importance of the family in most Asian cultures, how can the family structure be used for the spiritual growth of the individual family members?

These questions are surfacing because there seems to be a tendency to rely more heavily on Western psychological models and processes not only in the training of psychologists and counselors, but also as a resource for pastoral counselors and spiritual directors. For instance, in the Philippines the American psychological models have been adopted for so long, and many of the categories which stress the individual self do not seem to fit the psychological make-up of the Filipino, who is more familial by nature. Many Filipino traits and attitudes stress the value of "belongingness" and loyalty to one's in-group, the importance of acceptance and affirmation by authority and outsiders, and the primacy of one's family, both nuclear and extended. These seem to militate against the strengthening of the individual self. Yet the renewal and growth of the Filipino do not lie solely in the use of Western psychological processes, although the latter might have valuable insights to offer. I believe this renewal and growth would depend on one's effort to discover the original genius of the Filipino culture by harnessing the positive aspects of one's traits and psychological orientations to make them work for, rather than against, one's wholistic growth.

For example, the Filipino trait called *pakikisama* ("belongingness" and loyalty to one's in-group) has acquired a pejorative meaning because of the strong social pressure that robs an individual of one's capacity to decide for oneself. However, *pakikisama* can become a positive value if it is modified to apply not only to one's small group but to the larger community as well. The positive aspects of this trait are better expressed by the word *bayanihan* or cooperative togetherness.

'Transference" and "Counter-transference" in the Multicultural Situation

In psychoanalytic understanding, transference is described as a reproduction of emotions relating to repressed experiences, especially of childhood, and a replacement of another person, such as the psychoanalyst, for the original object of the repressed impulses. Counter-transference is the psychoanalyst's unconscious response reaction to the client's transference.

Although spiritual direction is not psychoanalysis, it deals with the person's history as in psychoanalysis. Therefore, in the process of spiritual direction, feelings and memories may be evoked from the directee's unconscious as she or he interacts with God in prayer and with the person of the director. Repressed experiences come not only from one's personal history but also from the people's collective history. This is further complicated by cultural expectations that dictate how a person must relate in society.

An example of this type of expectation is the Asian hierarchical relationships in the family, which a Westerner who greatly values his or her personal freedom might find difficult to understand and accept for himself or herself. In structural hierarchical relationships where reciprocal responsibilities and obligations of senior and junior are carefully observed, any direct expression of contradictory opinion or anger, particularly by the junior, is considered a serious transgression. Thus an Asian counselee or directee who is immersed only in his or her culture would automatically operate in a structural hierarchical way in relating to his or her counselor or director.

It is not enough for spiritual directors to be aware that various levels of repression have to be dealt with in the spiritual direction process itself. They also need to be skilled in understanding and in processing the psychological orientation of their culturally different directee.

One particular help spiritual directors can avail themselves of is training in cross-cultural counseling. In this particular training, counselors are helped to develop a special skill called "interpathy." Cross-culturalist David Augsburger describes interpathy as "an intentional cognitive envisioning and affective experiencing of another's thoughts and feelings, even though the thoughts rise from another process of knowing, the values grow from another frame of moral reasoning, and the feelings spring from another basis of assumptions."[12]

How does one practice interpathy? Since it requires that one enter the other's world of assumptions, beliefs, and values and temporarily take them as one's own, "one must consciously bracket one's own beliefs, and believe what the other believes, see as the other sees, value what the other values, and feel the consequent feelings as the other feels them. Interpathy training must therefore be broad enough to include alternative worldviews."[13] For example, in the case I mentioned above about the Asian hierarchical system in the family, a culturally aware Western counselor or director, in practicing interpathy, must try to bracket first his or her own egalitarian and freedom-oriented values and beliefs and enter into the other's perspective in order to understand, feel, see, and believe the way the other does.

Considering the insights available to us through our knowledge of the culture's psychological and spiritual processes, we are thus challenged to look into alternative structures of spiritual direction.

Alternative Structures of Spiritual Direction

In the Christian tradition, spiritual direction has usually followed the one-on-one structure in the interaction between the director and the directee. Considering the psychological orientation and mind-set of a particular culture, we begin to ask if such a structure would be effective all the time. What are alternative models of spiritual direction, besides the classic one-on-one model, that are proving helpful in Asian situations?

I am seeing answers emerging to these questions. For instance, in the Filipino culture, it is not altogether unusual for someone who is coming for counseling or spiritual direction for the first time to take along a close friend to the session. Although my Western-trained mind was not open to this practice in the past, I allowed it on several occasions for the sake of the counselee/directee. I realized that the Filipino trait called *hiya*, the notion of shame, especially in situations where there is potential for embarrassment,[14] was very strong in the person. The only way this person could break through this barrier was to have someone, usually a very close friend, support him or her emotionally and spiritually during the first stages of counseling or spiritual direction (usually during the first session). In this situation, the friend (who himself or herself had benefited from spiritual direction) was there to encourage the directee to be honest and open and to provide a supportive presence. The succeeding sessions would revert to the one-on-one structure.

I am not saying that this should be taken as a standard model, but considering the culture, a structure such as this could be allowed, especially if it is helpful to the directee.

Two other alternative structures are also appearing. They are the "Home Retreats" (an adaptation of the "At Home Retreats" started by American

Cenacle sister, Mary Sullivan, r.c., and Dot Horstman) and the BEC (Basic Ecclesial Community) or "base group model." Both have a familial atmosphere. For example, in some dioceses in the Philippines, the "Home Retreat" has been given to BEC couples as part of the deepening phase of the spiritual formation program within the basic communities. It has evidently been received enthusiastically.

A type of spiritual direction occurs when the retreat facilitator/spiritual director sees the participating couples (about four or five of them) for their weekly sharing and points for prayer. In turn, the couples making the retreat are adding a certain depth to their commitment when they return to their bigger BEC cells. Since this is still in the experimental stage, it needs further study and exploration, but I see the evolving structure as a relevant response to the family-centered culture of the Filipino.

The base group model is something I personally have tried, especially with the ANV (Active Non-Violence) group I was part of in 1985–1987. Most of the group members were laborers and factory workers who belonged to the urban poor. I had asked to be part of the group after I attended the ANV basic seminar. As a base group, we met weekly for faith sharing and discussions on how we have lived the ANV challenge in our home or convent and work situation. These meetings enabled our group to develop a trusting relationship with one another and to reach a certain level of spiritual affinity. On occasion I would be asked to direct a smaller group (five members) from the same base group for deepening sessions. We did this with great regularity every week for almost six months. As I reflect on this experience of directing the group, I would say that what I did was spiritual direction, for I directed the group the way I would an individual, except perhaps for the following.

As the person directing the group, I asked each one to listen deeply and prayerfully with me to the faith stories of each member of the small group. Since a certain level of trust and spiritual affinity was present, it was easier for each one to share more openly, deeply, and honestly with the others.

After each one had had an opportunity to share where she or he was in her or his faith and prayer life, her or his response to individual religious experiences, and how these affect perceptions and responses to everyday life, I shared with them briefly how I experienced God in my life. I felt it was important for the group to know that I was one with them and that we were all companions in our passover in the Lord. I was also aware that they looked at me as one who could guide them in their journey to God.

While listening to each one, I would ask for clarification when needed and show empathy or interpathy, depending on the situation. This taught the group how and what to share and enabled them to enter into their own process.

After each sharing, I would try to give a brief synthesis of where the group was and asked that we spend a few moments of silence to listen to where God's Spirit might be directing us individually and as a group.

I would invite each one to briefly share whatever "lights" she or he might have received from the Holy Spirit before giving my own suggestions for reflection and prayer to the individuals (if they needed different points) and to the group.

Based on the above experience, I see that the following areas need to be considered and emphasized in group spiritual direction:

Preparation. In the above case, preparation for the deepening sessions consisted of participation in a weekend retreat-seminar on Active Non-Violence and the weekly base group meeting.

Commitment. It was made clear at the outset that only those who could commit themselves regularly to this ongoing deepening session should participate. Commitment on their part consisted of their willingness to set aside at least three hours every other week for the sessions and at least fifteen minutes of quiet reflection and/or Scripture reading each day.

Number. I limited the deepening group to a maximum of six people, all of whom came from the 25–30 members of our ANV base group. They, in turn, became leaven in the bigger base community.

These emerging answers and directions need further study and development. However, for retreat and spiritual directors to utilize such structures more effectively, they have to be skilled in multicultural awareness and communication. This will be explored more fully in the next section, so as to spark more answers and ideas for the training of spiritual directors.

MULTICULTURAL AWARENESS AND COMMUNICATION

Multicultural awareness and communication are important in a world that is becoming progressively unified due to rapid advancements in communication, economic and even cultural interdependence, and mutual political influence. Anyone involved in the ministry of helping and guiding people therefore has a professional obligation to become multicultural herself or himself. What kind of programs and experiences must be designed for spiritual directors so they can be helped to become multicultural persons?

In the area of awareness and communication, recurring concerns and issues have surfaced in multicultural situations. If the saying that "meanings are not in words but are in people" is true, how then does a particular group of people attribute meanings to words and communicate such meanings? What are the structures of communication in a culture? How are negative feelings and emotions dealt with? What are the kinds of communication barriers in multicultural situations? How are we to deal with them?

The most invaluable help for spiritual directors in dealing with these concerns is to learn the language of the people. Although not everyone has a gift for languages, the process of learning itself, even if one can never be proficient in the language, is an invaluable way of learning from the culture and people. Theologian Jose de Mesa once commented that "mere translation cannot be a substitute for listening to the culture in its own terms because every language has its own genius, its own distinctiveness, its own special character."[15] In addition, each language has its own genius, its own grammatical patterns, its own peculiar idioms, its own areas of vocabulary strength, and its own weakness and limitations.[16] All these should be respected. They do not, however, repudiate in any way the need for translations, which are necessary for multicultural communication and sharing of insights.

Besides learning the language, spiritual directors can participate in experiential programs and workshops that can be adapted to suit their needs. One particular seminar is based on Pierre Casse's book, *Training for the Cross-Cultural Mind*, which has been modified for communications training by international organizations and corporations. Some of the exercises in his book would be well-suited for the ongoing education of those in the helping ministry. Certainly the immersion or exposure experience mentioned earlier would also be an excellent practicum for multicultural awareness and communication.

Spiritual directors could also benefit from learning specific methods of listening to culture, such as Schreiter's semiotic method[17] and Meland's "appreciative awareness" approach to culture.[18] These methods require the listener to have at least some knowledge of the language and culture.

There are simpler ways of honing people's multicultural awareness. For instance, Pedersen's "Drawing Your Culture"[19] can be used for individual or group processes. The following are extracts from his explanation of this activity that may be adapted to suit one's situation:

Sometimes our verbal facility in describing our culture betrays us by abstracting the less rational and more emotional aspects of our cultural influences. By drawing the symbols that describe what our culture means, it is possible to escape from the preconceived format we usually use to describe our identity.

. . . Ask each individual to spend about 5–20 minutes (or more depending on the situation)[20] drawing her culture. Participants may draw pictures of events in their lives that have influenced them in their culture. They may also draw symbols that are particularly meaningful in their culture. They may draw any combination of designs, doodles, or lines that have meaning to them in terms of their culture. They may not, however, write any words on their paper.

. . . This exercise is useful for articulating some of the nonverbal, symbolic, or less rational aspects of our culture that are often difficult to describe in words.

The exercise is summarized in the following manner:
Participant Objectives:
1. To draw the figures or symbols important to their cultural identity;
2. To explain or express the figures or symbols they have drawn to other members of a small group; and

3. To listen and understand the figures or symbols other members of a small
   group have identified as important to their cultural identity.

Learning Objective:
Our cultural identity contains nonverbal, nonrational, and symbolic elements
that are difficult to express using language.

I have made it a point to adapt and use the above exercise with anyone
from another culture or subculture whom I direct in a retreat or to whom
I provide ongoing spiritual direction. From my experience in directing
Asians of different cultural backgrounds, the initial sessions are difficult.
Asians are often reticent to talk about their personal lives, much less about
their inner journey in prayer.

Using the above exercise has served the following purposes: as a way of
loosening up the atmosphere for open sharing, since most have found it to
be a nonthreatening activity; and as a tool for getting information about
the ways by which they perceive their sociocultural and religious environments and influences. The interaction usually becomes easier once they
have begun to share through symbols and images what they consider important to their identity and spiritual journey. The exercise gives the director
some insights into the other's culture. For instance, a Thai woman whom
I directed in an eight-day retreat commented that the exercise enabled her
to become aware, at the very beginning of her retreat, that she had been
gifted with a rich spiritual heritage because of the Buddhist and Christian
influences in her life and culture, for example, the animistic rituals of popular religiosity in her country.[21] I was then able to encourage her to tap
those resources to enhance her prayer life. It was interesting to note that
one of the symbols she drew about her culture expressed the Asian hierarchical structure in family, religion, and society. I was mindful of this at
the outset, being Asian myself. Such information, I think, would be particularly helpful for a non-Asian director to increase his or her awareness of
the dynamics in the director–directee relationship.

Undoubtedly there are many other ways of learning to be multicultural
persons. What we have included in this study are those that have direct
bearing on the ministry of retreat and spiritual direction.

In summary, we have focused on three areas worth examining and considering in designing and developing an ongoing program of education for
spiritual directors in multicultural situations. These are: inculturation, multicultural psycho-spiritual processes, and multicultural awareness and communication. In addressing each of the above areas, we raised further
concerns, questions and issues challenging us to explore creative ways of
addressing them. In the discussion, we have seen answers emerging drawn
from the experiences and insights of those engaged in multicultural ministries.

Lastly, our inquiry has demonstrated that in our multicultural world the spiritual director must listen not only to the directee's religious experience but also to the culture that informs and shapes his or her perceptions and responses to life.

NOTES

1. Marcello Azevedo, SJ, *Inculturation and the Challenges of Modernity* (Rome: Centre of Cultures and Religion, Pontifical Gregorian University, 1982), pp. 7–8.

2. Robert Schreiter, C.PP.S., *Constructing Local Theologies* (Maryknoll, N.Y.: Orbis Books, 1986), pp. 5–6.

3. Susana Jose, *San Juan de la Cruz Today* (Quezon City, Philippines: Carmelite Monastery of St. Therese, 1990), p. 71.

4. Aloysius Pieris, SJ, "Toward an Asian Theology of Liberation: Some Religio-Cultural Guidelines," *Vidyajyoti* (July 1979): 262–63.

5. Vitaliano Gorospe, SJ, *Filipino Values Revisited* (Manila: National Book Store, Inc., 1988), p. 70.

6. Ibid., p. 72.

7. This poem is quoted by Choan-Seng Song in his article, "Freedom of Christian Theology for Asian Cultures: Celebrating the Inauguration of the Programme for Theology and Cultures in Asia," *Asia Journal of Theology* 3 (April, 1989): 85.

8. Gorospe, p. 68.

9. This addition is mine.

10. Federation of Asian Bishops Conference, "Emerging Priorities and Perspectives," *East Asian Pastoral Review* 25 (No. 4, 1988): 431–32.

11. Alan Roland, *In Search of Self in India and Japan: Toward a Cross-Cultural Psychology* (Princeton, N.J.: Princeton University Press, 1988), p. 4.

12. David Augsburger, *Pastoral Counseling Across Cultures* (Philadelphia: The Westminster Press, 1986), p. 13. Here the author asserts that awareness of one's culture can free one to disconnect identity from cultural externals and to live on the boundary, crossing over and coming back with increasing freedom.

13. Ibid., p. 14.

14. But in the Filipino cultures there is more to *hiya* than just "saving face." It is considered both a feeling and a value. As a feeling, it is connected to one's familial self. As a value, it is linked to one's sense of dignity and respectability as a person.

15. Jose de Mesa, *In Solidarity with the Culture* (Quezon City, Philippines: Maryhill School of Theology, 1987), p. 263.

16. Ibid., p. 263.

17. The third chapter of his book, *Constructing Local Theologies*, explains this method in greater detail.

18. de Mesa, pp. 27ff.

19. Paul Pedersen, *A Handbook for Developing Multicultural Awareness* (American Association for Counseling and Development, 1988), pp. 36–37.

20. Adaptation mine. In a directed retreat situation, I would give the person 15–20 minutes and encourage her or him to do this in a reflective and meditative mood.

21. Theologians in Asia consider that a certain kind of animism can still be used for deeper spirituality, i.e., animism as a "signal of transcendence which points to the presence of the 'holy' and preserves the person's sense of God" (Gorospe, p. 69).

Contributors

ANN BELLIVEAU, SSA, is a Sister of St. Anne, originally from Massachusetts, who has ministered in Chile for the past ten years. She brings experience in education, therapy, formation, and spiritual direction to the people of Santiago, Chile, where she resides.

TERRENCE P. CHARLTON, SJ, hails from Indianapolis. He received his Ph.D. in systematic theology from Boston College and has taught at Xavier University, Cincinnati. After serving on the formation team at the Jesuit novitiate in Detroit, he was a staff member of the Centre for Spiritual Renewal in Kumasi, Ghana. He presently teaches systematic theology at Hekima College, Nairobi, Kenya.

JOAN CONRAD, SSND, earned masters' degrees in both music education and applied linguistics and has taught in high schools in the United States and in Japan. She completed the program of the Institute for Spiritual Leadership in Chicago and has worked in spiritual development for the past sixteen years.

JUDETTE A. GALLARES, rc, a Cenacle sister from the Philippines, is actively involved in the ministry of retreats and spiritual direction. She has done vocation and formation work for her congregation, was ministry coordinator at the Cenacle Retreat House in Quezon City, Philippines, and has given retreats and seminars in Singapore, Thailand, and the United States. She holds a M.A. in Religion and Religious Education from Fordham University and a Certificate in Biblical Spirituality from the Catholic Theological Union (Chicago).

ANTHONY J. GITTINS, CSSp, was born in Manchester, England, and is a member of the Congregation of the Holy Ghost (Spiritans). He holds a Ph.D. in social anthropology from the University of Edinburgh and lived with the Mende people in Sierra Leone for eight years. Professor of Theological Anthropology at the Catholic Theological Union in Chicago, he also works regularly in a shelter for homeless women.

ADELE J. GONZALEZ earned her M.A. in Religious Studies from Barry University, Miami. Postgraduate studies have included the Shalom Spiritual Guidance Program in Washington, D.C. She is presently Associate Director of the Office of Lay Ministry of the Archdiocese of Miami, Florida, and is known throughout the United States for her involvement in Evangelization and Lay Ministry in multicultural settings.

MARINA HERRERA, Ph.D., is a consultant, lecturer, writer, and facilitator of intercultural/interracial dialogue. She has helped dioceses, parishes, seminaries, and schools throughout the United States define new dynamics for communication, collaboration, and celebration in a multicultural setting. Her articles have appeared in more than a dozen journals and her book *LASER: Creating Unity in Diversity* (1985) tells the story of a national project to facilitate intercultural exchanges in twelve Catholic dioceses throughout the United States.

CONRAD C. HOOVER, CO, is a priest of the Oratory of St. Philip Neri in Rock Hill, South Carolina, where he serves on the retreat team, teaches theology, and ministers to persons with AIDS.

PADRAIC LEONARD, CSSp, is a member of the Holy Spirit Congregation. Born in Ireland, he studied theology and was ordained in Fribourg, Switzerland. After teaching high school for ten years in Ireland, he went to Brazil in 1966. In 1974 he defended a doctoral thesis on the thought of Dom Helder Camara at the Saint Louis University Divinity School. For the past ten years he has been working with the Conference of Religious of Brazil in the field of spirituality.

GREGORY LOURENS of Cape Town, South Africa, is married to Marianne; they have two sons, Jon-Luke and Vincent. As a member of the Christian Life Communities, he has been actively involved in the area of spiritual formation and has been engaged in the ministry of spiritual direction for the past eleven years.

DOMINIC MARUCA, SJ, holds a doctorate in Ascetical and Mystical Theology, has served as master of novices for the Maryland Province, and is presently teaching at the Institute of Spirituality of the Pontifical Gregorian University in Rome. He has worked with priests and religious in North and South America, the Caribbean, Africa, Asia, and Europe for thirty years.

THOMAS H. O'GORMAN, SJ, is presently the director of the Jesuit Tertianship for East Asia. From 1984 to 1989 he was the director of the East Asian Pastoral Institute in Manila. He has directed Ignatian retreats in the Philippines, Singapore, Hong Kong, Japan, and the United States and has engaged in clergy renewal courses in Korea and Australia as well as the Philippines. He holds a doctorate from the Gregorian University in Rome, where he specialized in spiritual theology.

LILY QUINTOS, rc, holds a doctorate in moral theology from the Catholic University of Louvain (Belgium). She has lectured and given retreats on four continents and has been a visiting Professor of Theology and Asian Culture at the Pacific School of Religion as a Henry Luce Scholar. She will be visiting professor of moral theology at St. Joseph's School of Theology, University of Alberta, Edmonton, Canada, 1991–1992.

SUSAN RAKOCZY, IHM, holds a doctorate in theology from the Catholic University of America. Her cross-cultural experience has been in Africa, where she first ministered in Ghana as a staff member of the Centre for Spiritual Renewal, Kumasi, from 1983 to 1988 and is now lecturing in systematic theology and spirituality at St. Joseph's Theological Institute, Cedara, South Africa. Her articles have appeared in *Liturgy, Missiology, Review for Religious,* and *Spirituality Today.*

CARL F. STARKLOFF, SJ, who has worked among native peoples in the United States and Canada for over thirty years, is presently associate professor of systematic and pastoral theology at Regis College in the Toronto School of Theology. He is also an instructor in theological education by extension at Anishinabe Spiritual Centre in northern Ontario and has published some forty articles in related areas.

BERNARD WARD, MCCJ, is a Comboni Missionary. He earned an STB from the Missionary Institute of London and masters' degrees from Louvain and Durham University (counseling). After pastoral work in Malawi he trained and worked as a retreat director at St. Beuno's, Wales, and also trained in therapeutic community practice at the Royal College of Nursing. He currently does parish work and spiritual direction in South Africa.